# Neustadt Ontario and Area in Colour Photos, Saving Our History One Photo at a Time

Photography
by Barbara Raué
2015

Series Name:
Cruising Ontario

Book 106: Neustadt

Cover photo: Robert and Janice Polfuss' house, see Page 10

# Series Name: Cruising Ontario
## Saving Our History One Photo at a Time
## in colour photos

# Other Books by Barbara Raue

Coins of Gold

Arrows, Indians and Love

The Life and Times of Barbara
Volume 1: Inventions That Have Enhanced My Life
Volume 2: Entertainment That I Have Enjoyed
Volume 3: East Coast Trips
Volume 4: Olympics Have Always Intrigued Me
Volume 5: Wonders of the World
Volume 6: Caribbean Cruises We Have Enjoyed
Volume 7: Animals
Volume 8: Storms and Other Major Disasters in My Lifetime
Volume 9: Wars, Terrorist Attacks and Major Disasters

The Cromwell Family Book

Laura Secord Discovered

Daddy Where Are You?

Visit Barbara's website to view all of her books
http://barbararaue.ca

# Neustadt

Neustadt is a community in the municipality of West Grey in Grey County in southern Ontario. The village is located south of Hanover on Grey Road 10 and north of Guelph and Kitchener. Neustadt is a picturesque rural Ontario village with German roots and a village history full of vibrant farming culture.

The village's name is of German origin and it translates to "new town". It was founded in 1856 by David Winkler, a settler from Germany. He purchased 400 acres from the government, laid out the town-site, dammed Meux Creek and built a sawmill. A flour mill and grist mill were also erected near the dam the following year. Many other German speaking settlers began arriving immediately. Winkler was the founder of many other institutions, including opening the first post office in town in the year 1857. Later he became a Justice of the Peace and Reeve of Normanby Township.

John Weinert, a saddle maker from Prussia, moved into Neustadt in 1859 and established a tannery on the north side of William Street. By 1861, he had added a boot and shoe factory and supplied footwear to the settlers. Henry Huether, an immigrant from Baden, Germany, constructed a wooden frame Brewery; a fire in 1859 destroyed it. The brewery was reconstructed in fieldstone and reopened in 1869. The brewery continued to be successful until 1916 when it became a creamery. For many years it remained empty until 1997 when it was reopened as Neustadt Springs Brewery which currently brews ten brands of beer.

In the early 1880s, the village saw its peak of development. The opening of a modern school and several new churches, businesses, and industries lead to a growth in population. Many years later, small businesses, farm equipment dealer, creameries, woolen mills, egg grading stations, some stores and later banks began to vanish. Each closure was critical to the village. Fewer attractions meant fewer visitors; the economy and population began to decline. In 2000, the Village of Neustadt with the Townships of Bentinck, Glenelg and Normanby, and the Town of Durham formed the Municipality of West Grey.

## Elmwood

West Grey is a township in western Ontario in Grey County spanning across the River Styx, the Rocky Saugeen River, the Beatty Saugeen River, and the South Saugeen River. Unlike most rural communities, West Grey maintains its own police force, the West Grey Police Service.

The Municipality of West Grey includes the community of Elmwood.

## Marmion

Chatsworth is a township in south-western Ontario in Grey County and is located at the headwaters of six rivers, the Styx, Saugeen, Sauble, Bighead, Spey, and Sydenham.

Desboro, Dornoch, Keady, Marmion, and Williamsford are some of the communities in Chatsworth Township.

# Desboro

Desboro is a community in Chatsworth Township, Grey County and is located south of Owen Sound and near the community of Chatsworth. Desboro is about 13 kilometres west of Chatsworth and Williamsford.

The first building in 1856 in the village of Desboro was a log school house. The area was originally called Brown's Corners, later Donnybrook, and then Desborough after a village in central England. The first house and store were built in 1866 by George Smith.

The Desboro hotel was built in 1869 and was one of the only rural taverns still operating in the township before it closed in 2011. The town hall was built in 1875 and enlarged to a two storey building in 1950.

# Williamsford

Williamsford is a village on the North Saugeen River in Grey County, Chatsworth Township. It is located on Highway 6 between Durham and Owen Sound.

Williamsford was first surveyed in 1858 comprising 400 acres in preparation for a railway which was to run from Toronto to Owen Sound. Each township was to contribute $40,000 to its construction. The post office was built in 1847 and the general store was built in the late 1800s.

It has a general store, post office, bookstore and restaurant housed in a historic grain mill. A small dam controls the North Saugeen River. It has several churches, and a community cemetery.

# Arkwright

Arkwright was an important community in the early days of Bruce County's history. First settled in the 1850s, it gained prominence as both a supply centre and busy stopping place along the stage route. At its height Arkwright boasted two hotels, two stores, a wagon shop, two blacksmiths and a physician. A sawmill was located close by. There was also a school and two Methodist churches. A post office that operated from 1857 to 1915 was located in one of the general stores. Arkwright also served as the seat of township government for many years.

Arkwright was a victim of declining rural population. Lack of a railway prevented it from attracting any major industries during the early days. With no industries or large businesses to sustain it, the hamlet gradually shut down. Today Arkwright is a small rural backwater with a handful of residents. It still contains a number of early structures including the hotel, town hall, schoolhouse and the church which are in use as private homes.

# Dobbinton

The Municipality of Arran–Elderslie is a township in Bruce County in western Ontario. The township is located at the headwaters of the Sauble River, and the Saugeen River forms the northwestern boundary.

The township includes the communities of Arkwright, Chesley, Dobbinton, Tara, and Williscroft, among others.

# Keady

Every Tuesday rain or shine, the farmer's market at Keady is open with up to 250 vendors selling a wide variety of produce ranging from Niagara peaches to deli meats, home baking, crafts and a broad assortment of other goods. There are livestock auctions beginning at 10 am. Keady is located at the intersection of Grey Roads 3 & 16.

# Tara

Tara, a community in southwestern Ontario within the municipality of Arran-Elderslie, is located on the Sauble River.

Richard Berford and John Hamilton were the first European settlers to survey lots for the village of Tara. The opening of the road from Southampton to Owen Sound in 1852 helped the early growth of the community, as the village is located approximately half-way in between the two larger towns.  Hamilton opened a hotel serving the incoming settlers of the surrounding townships. A post-office opened in 1862 with the name Eblana, which was changed the following year to Tara, after a town in County Meath, Ireland which served as the seat of Irish royalty.  In 1880, the local newspaper, *The Tara Leader* was published, and the following year the railroad was built to the community and the first locomotive arrived.

Among Tara's famous residents is former hockey legend Cyclone Taylor, a professional hockey player in the early 20th century.

# Williscroft

Williscroft had a post office, sawmill, flour and grist mill, cheese factory, store, blacksmith shops, Baptist Church, school and swimming hole in Snake Creek.

# Table of Contents

Neustadt

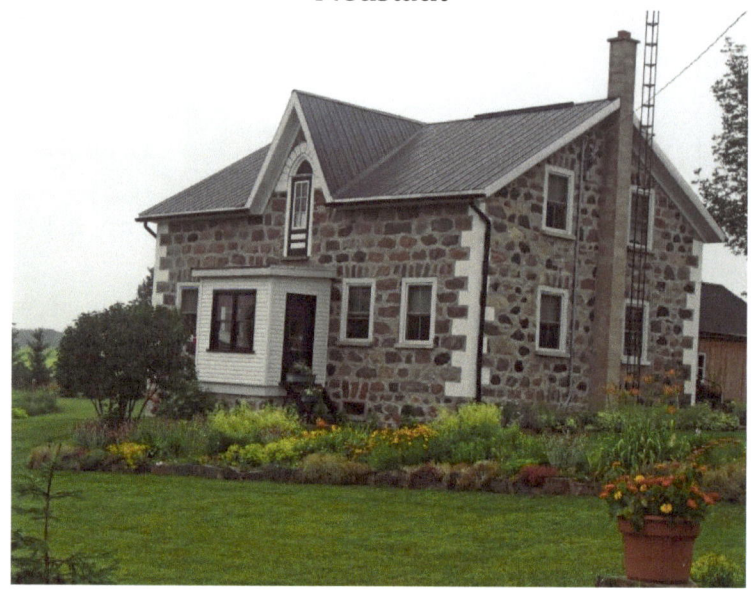

Robert and Janice Polfuss' house – Gothic Revival,
cobblestone, corner quoins

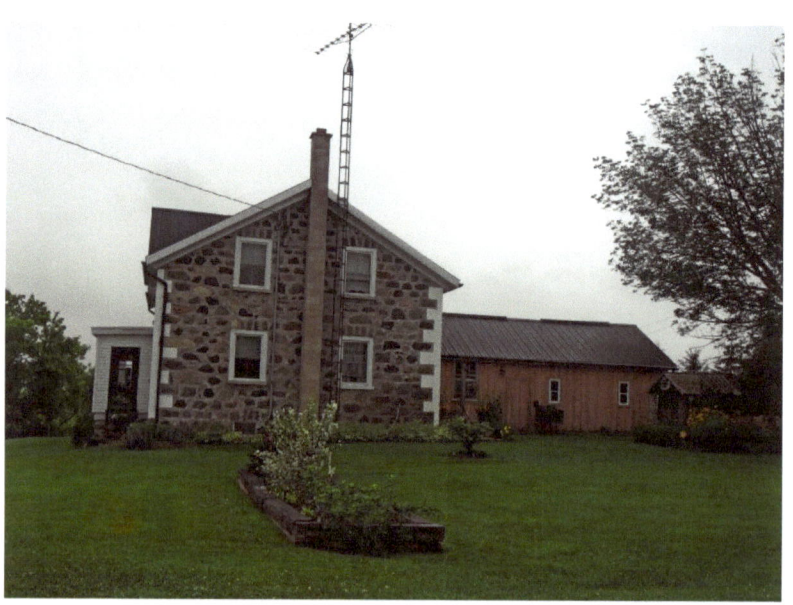

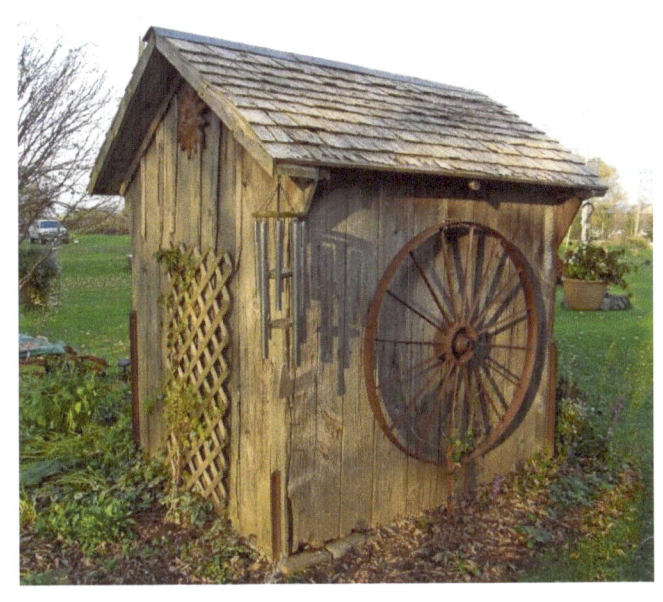

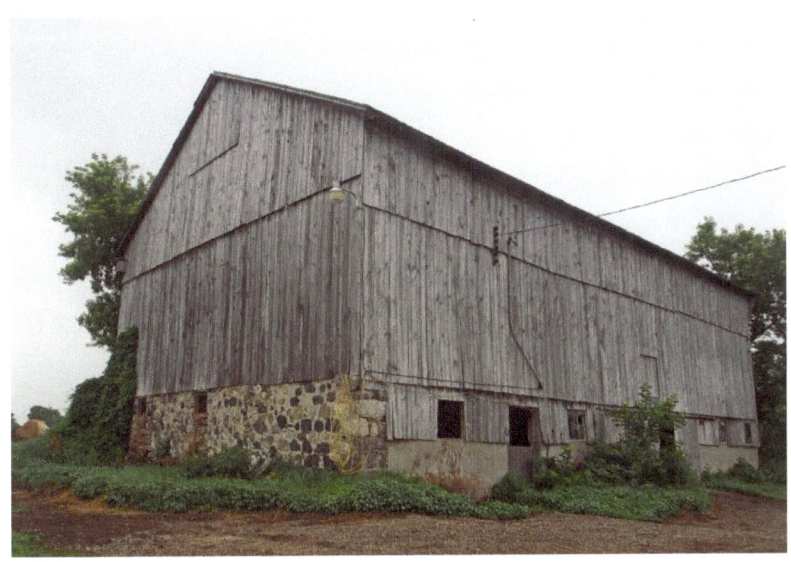

Cobblestone lower walls

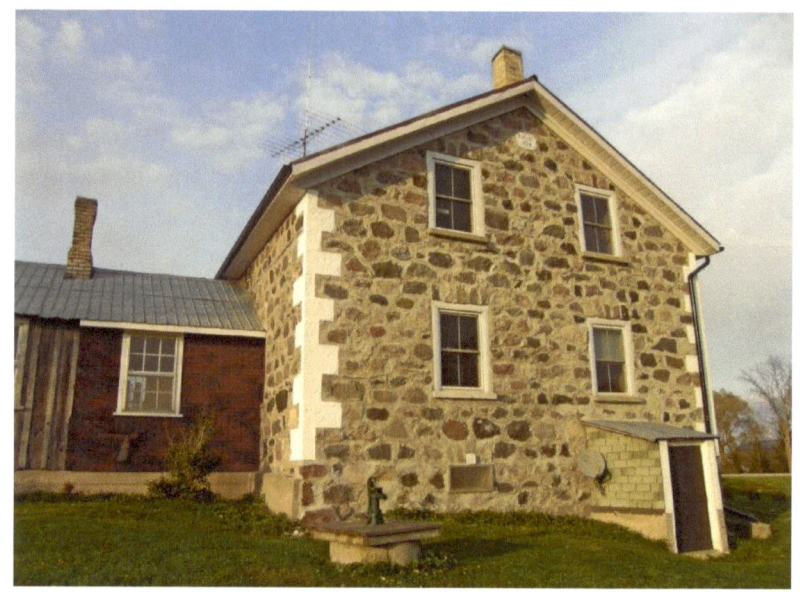

K. Kuhl – 1870 - Gothic - cobblestone

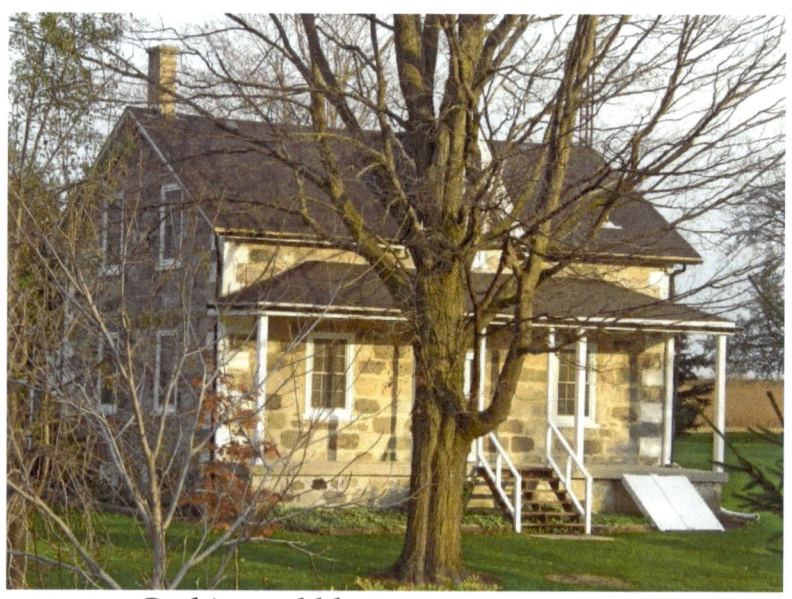

Gothic – cobblestone, corner quoins

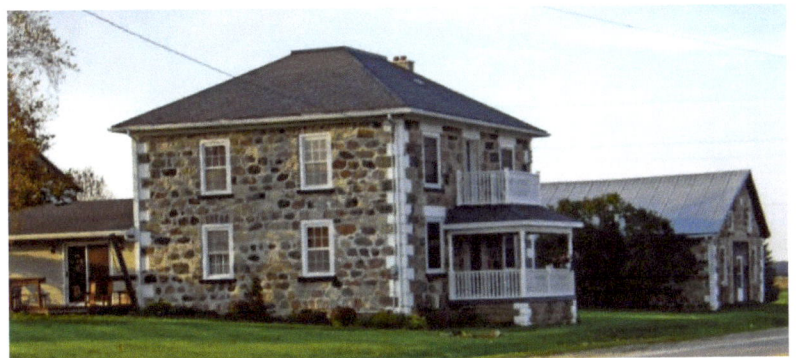

Italianate – cobblestone, corner quoins

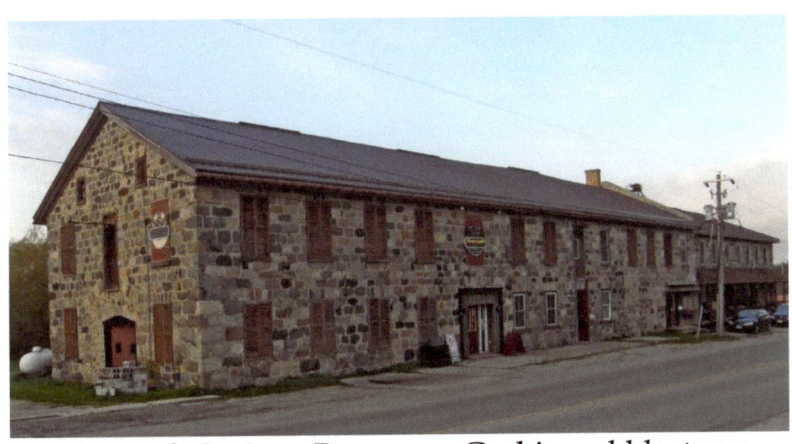

Neustadt Springs Brewery - Gothic, cobblestone

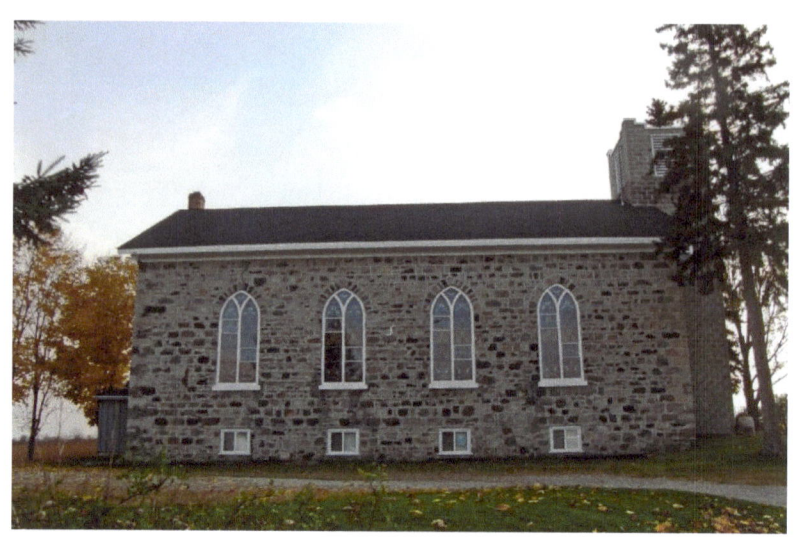

#461 - St. Peter's Evangelical Lutheran Church 1869

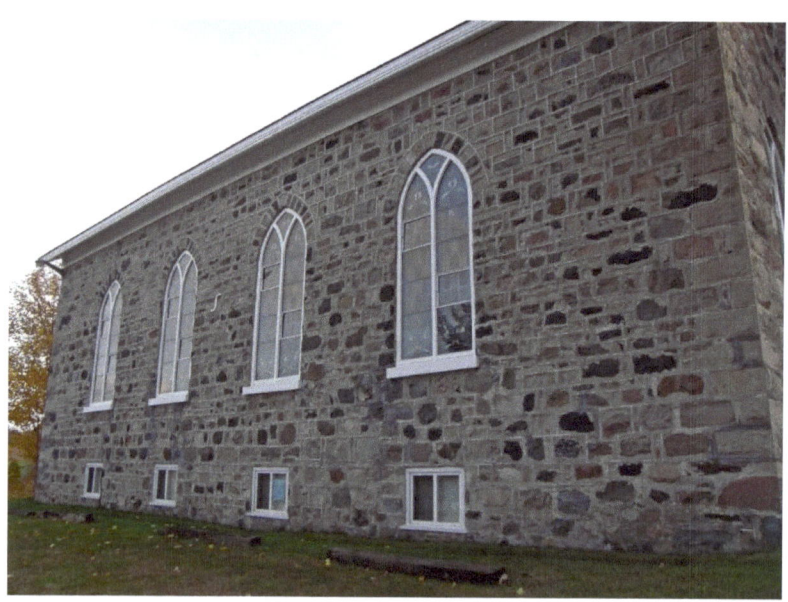

Cobblestone

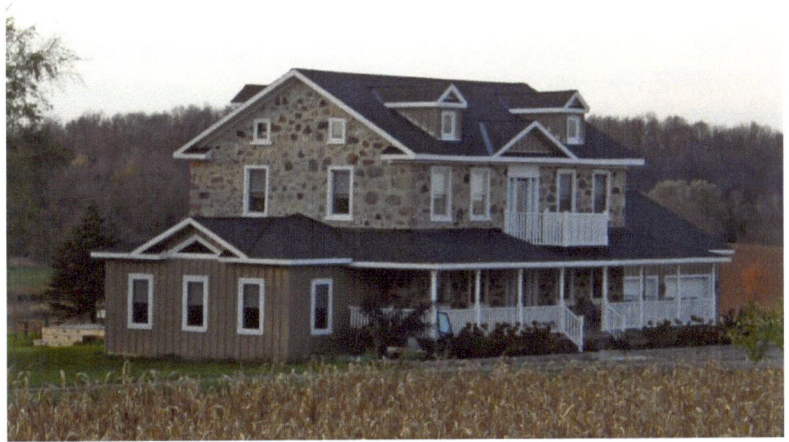

Gothic - cobblestone, cornice return on gable, dormers, balcony on second floor

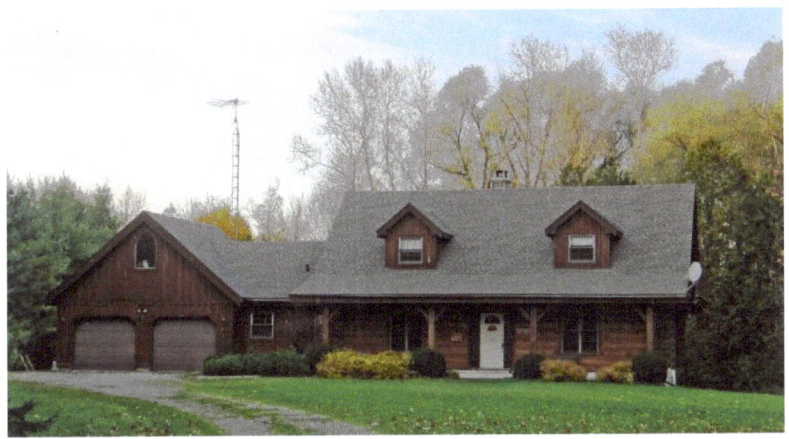

Log cabin, dormers

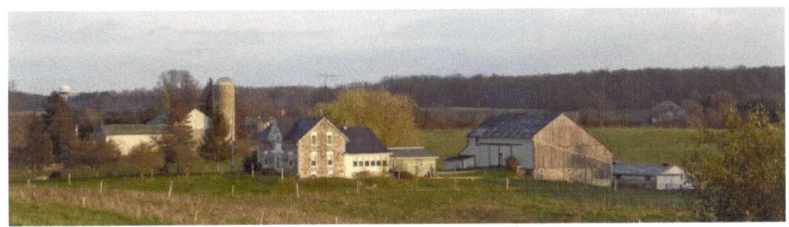

Farm – Gothic Revival, cobblestone

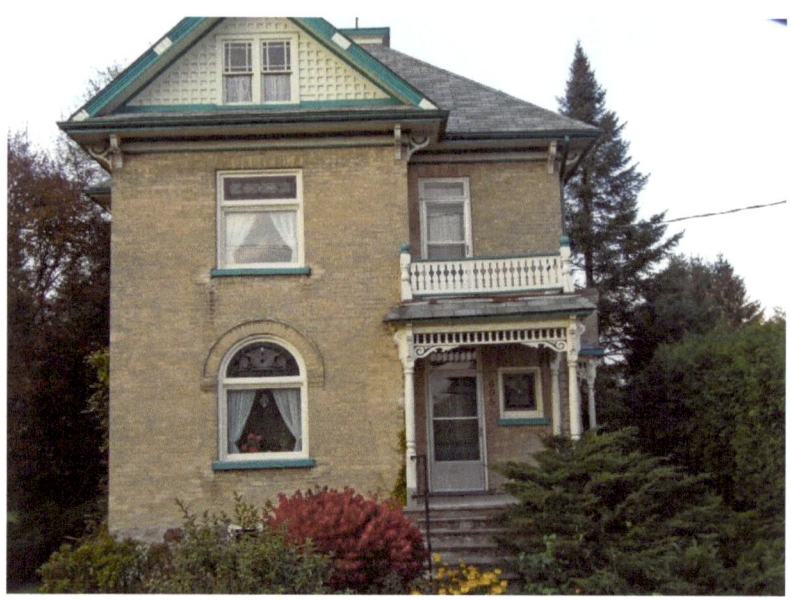

Edwardian, balcony on second floor

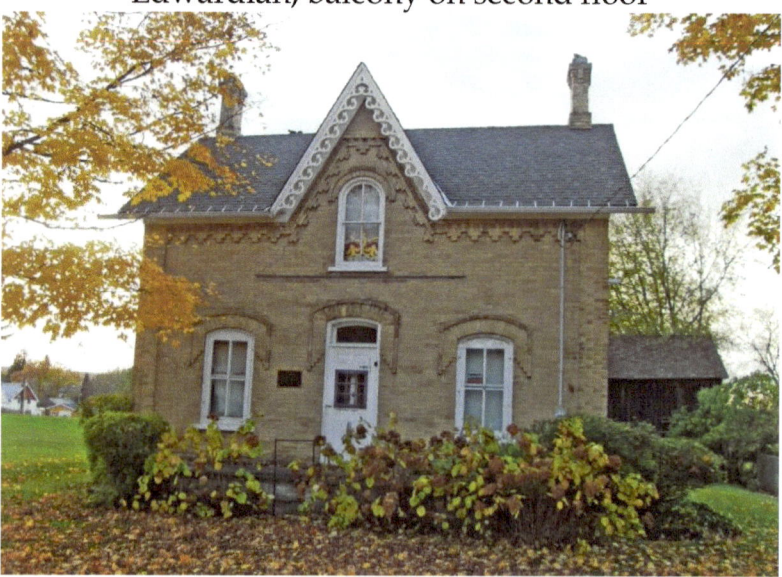

The Right Honourable John Diefenbaker, son of a local school teacher, was born in this house on September 18, 1895. A distinguished Parliamentarian, he was first elected to the House of Commons in 1940 and served as 13th Prime Minister of Canada, 1957-1963. Gothic Revival, verge board on gable.

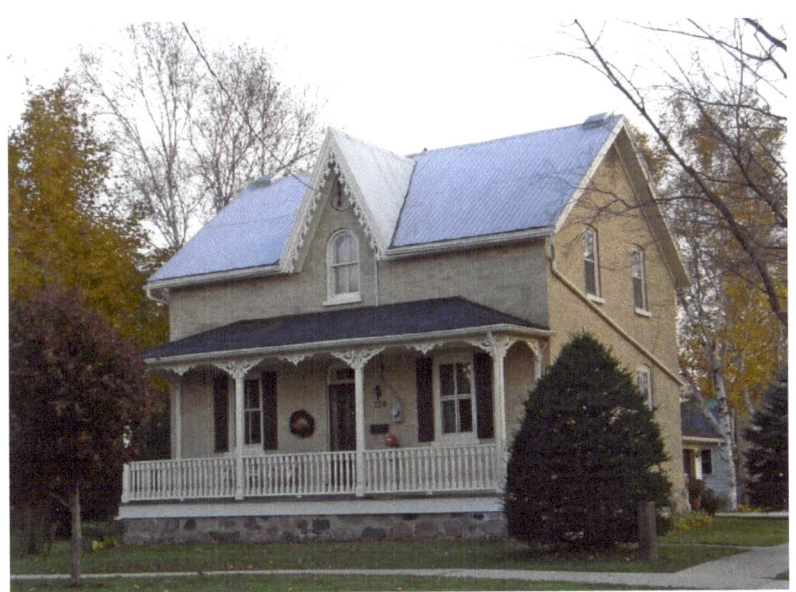

#720 – Gothic Revival, verge board trim on gable

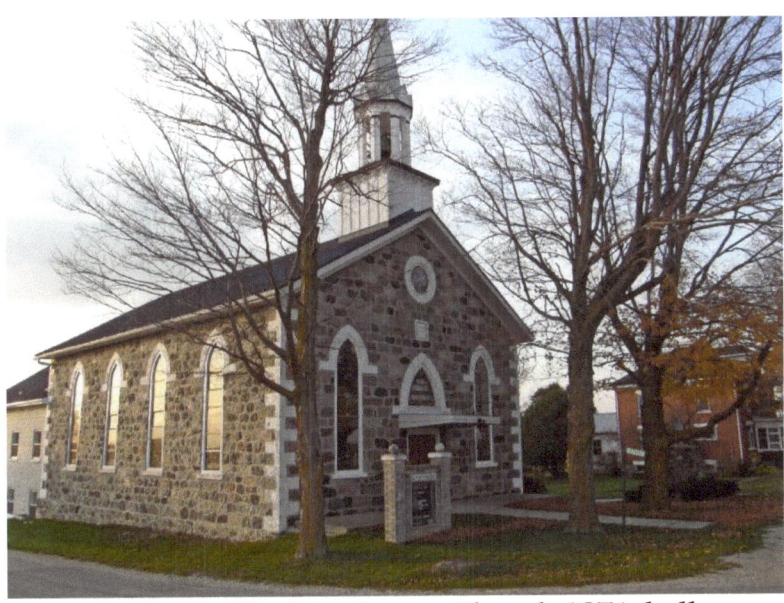

St. Paul's Evangelical Lutheran Church 1874, bell tower, corner quoins, cobblestone architecture

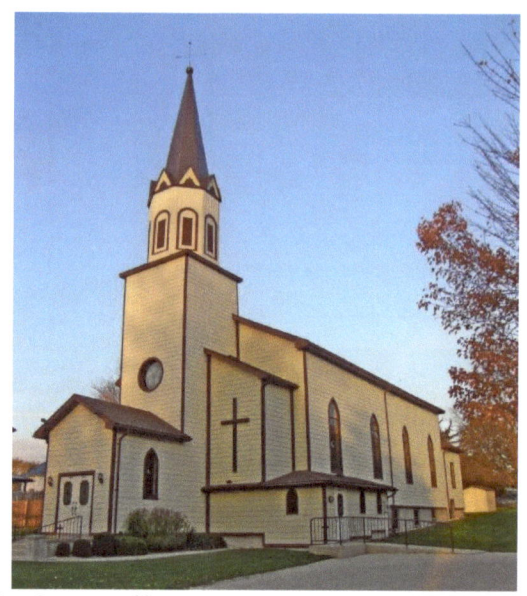

#379 - St. Paul's Evangelical Lutheran Church

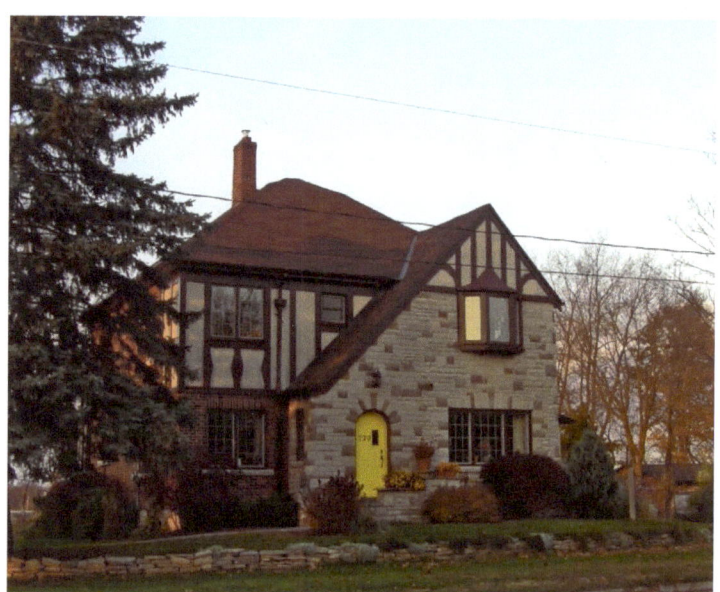

Tudor

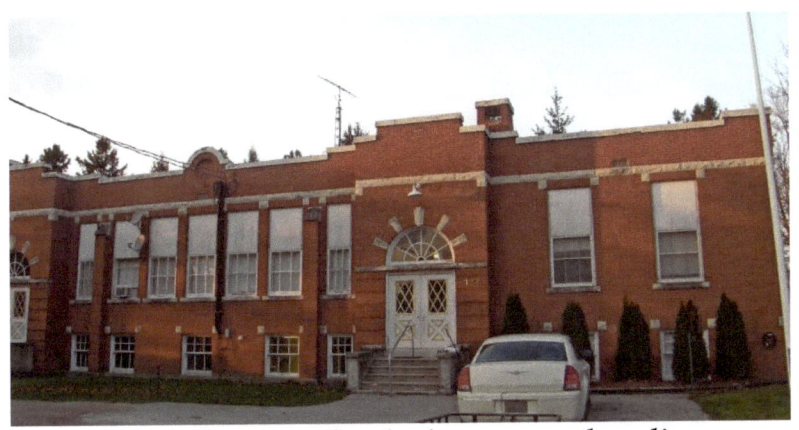

#127 – former school – buttresses, banding

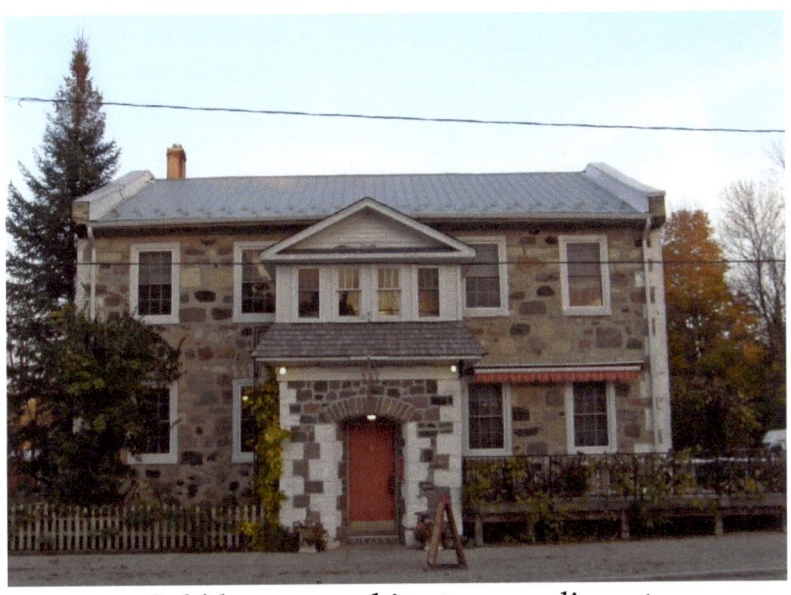

Cobblestone architecture, pediment

# Elmwood

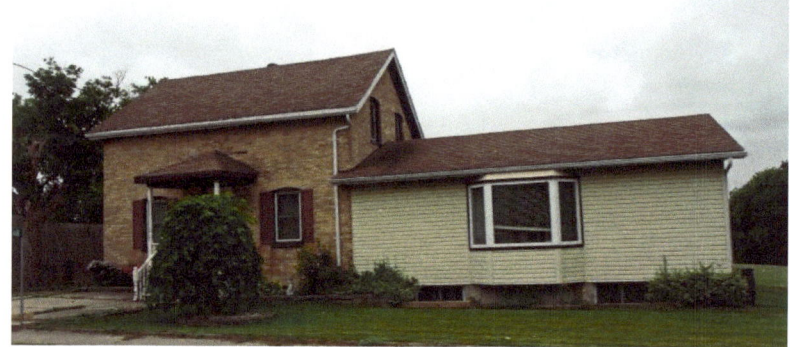

Gothic – end gable

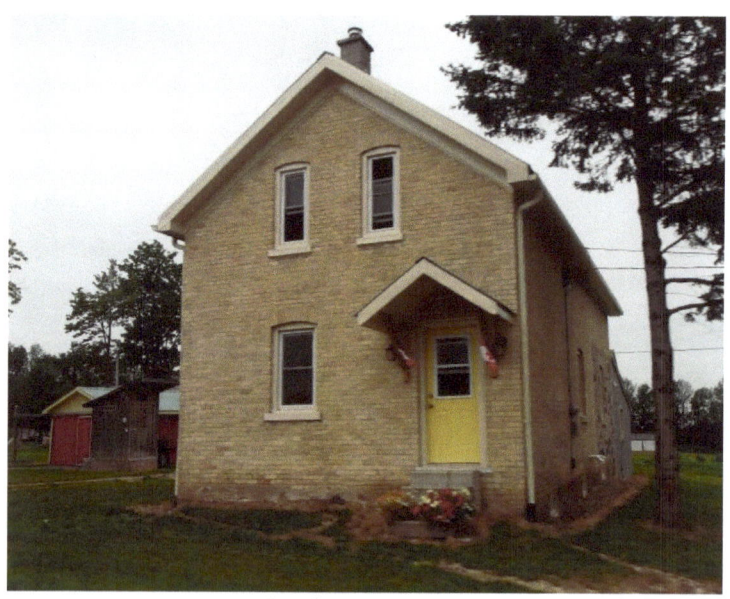

Gothic Revival

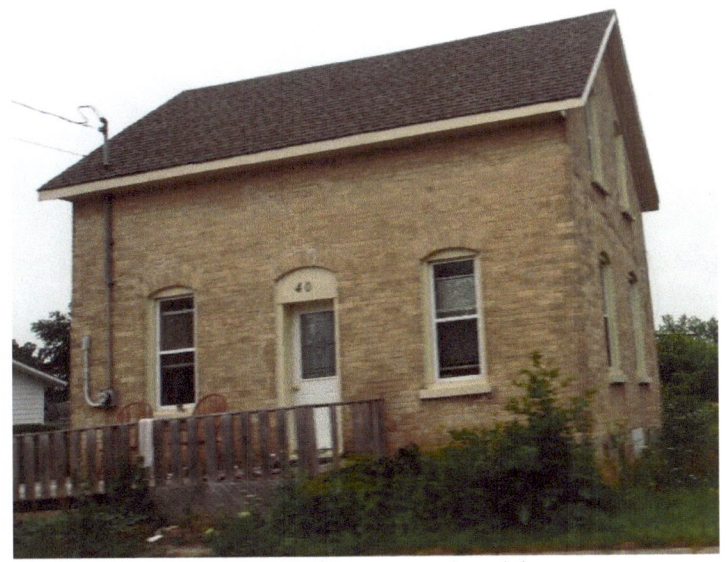

#40 – Gothic – end gable

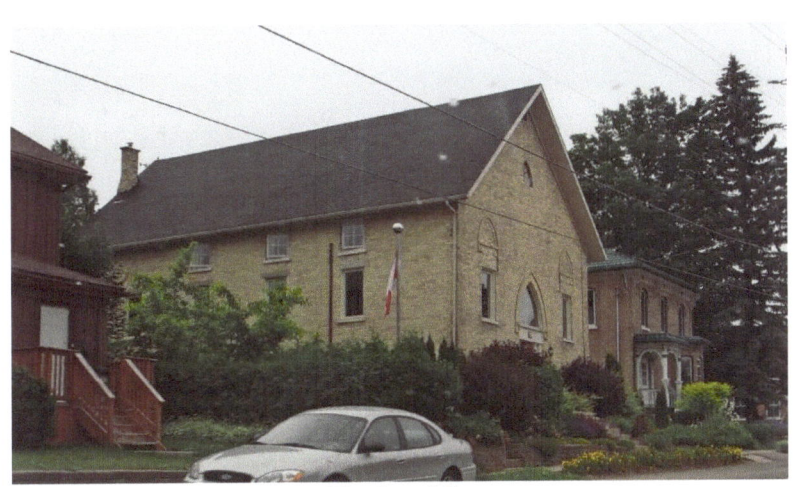

End gable

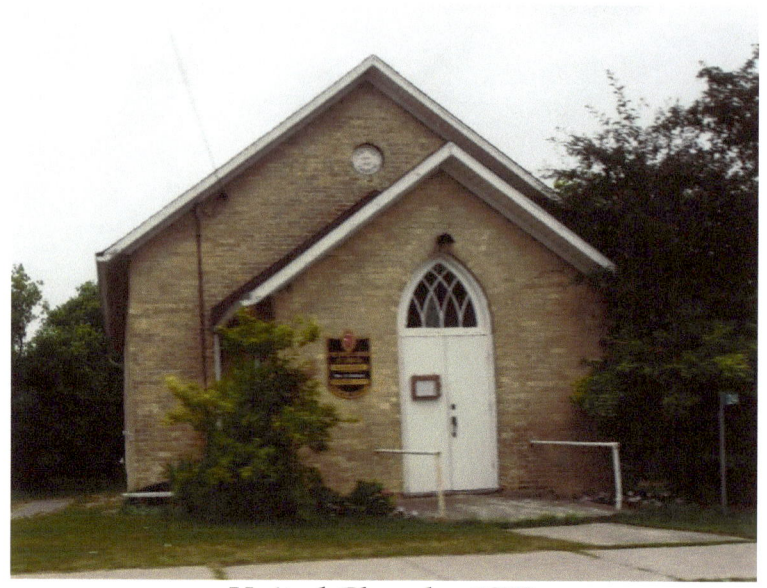

United Church - 1878

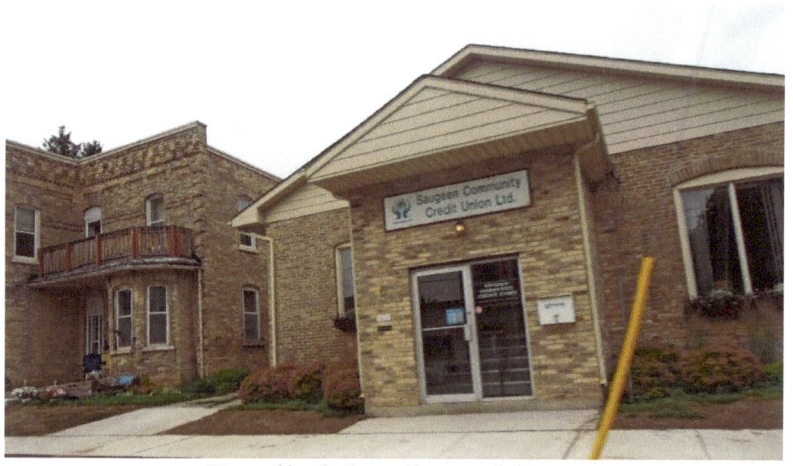

Bevelled dentil moulding,
2nd floor balcony above bay window

Desboro

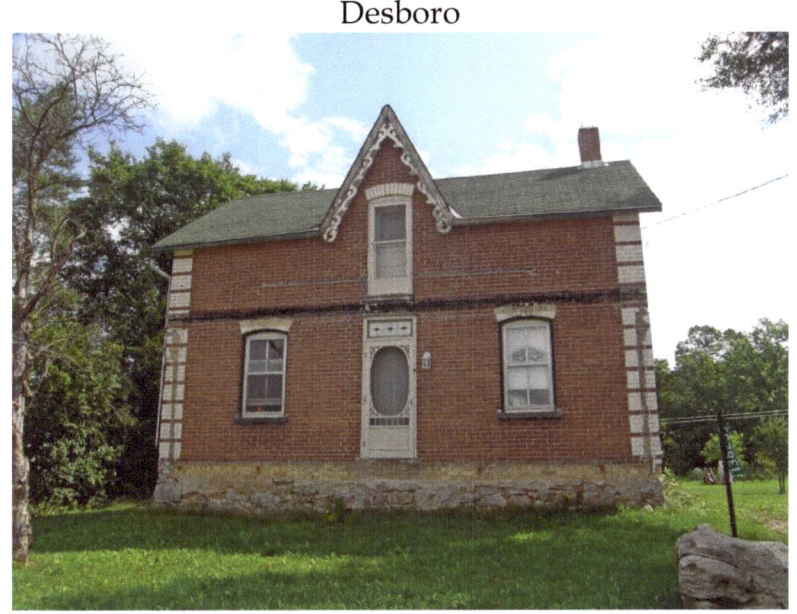

Gothic Revival, verge board trim on gable, corner quoins

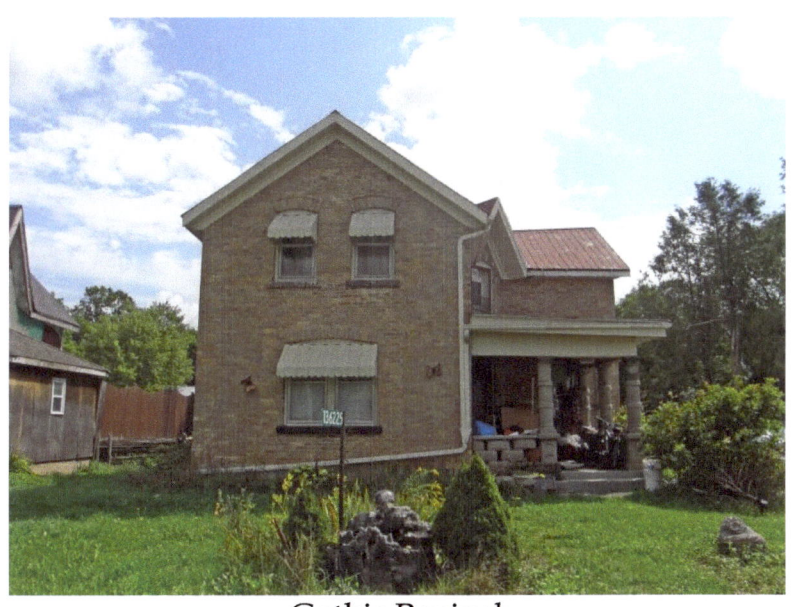

Gothic Revival

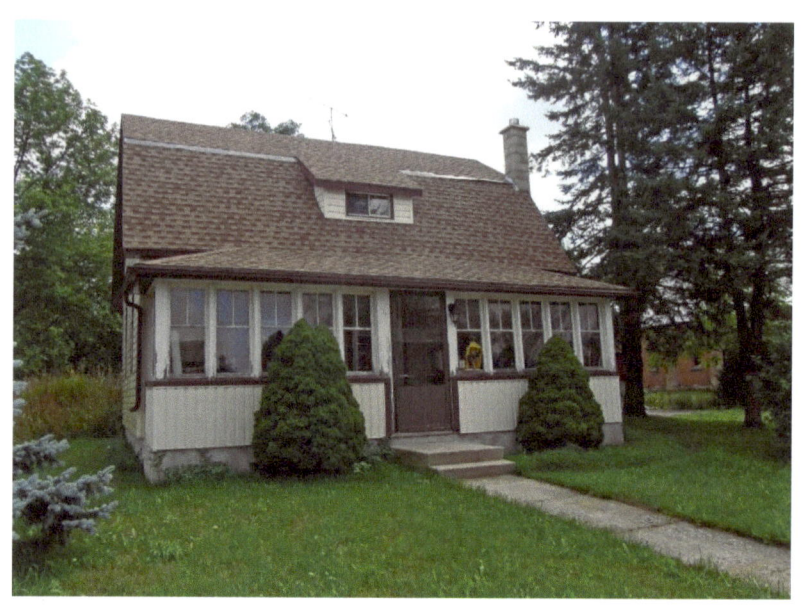

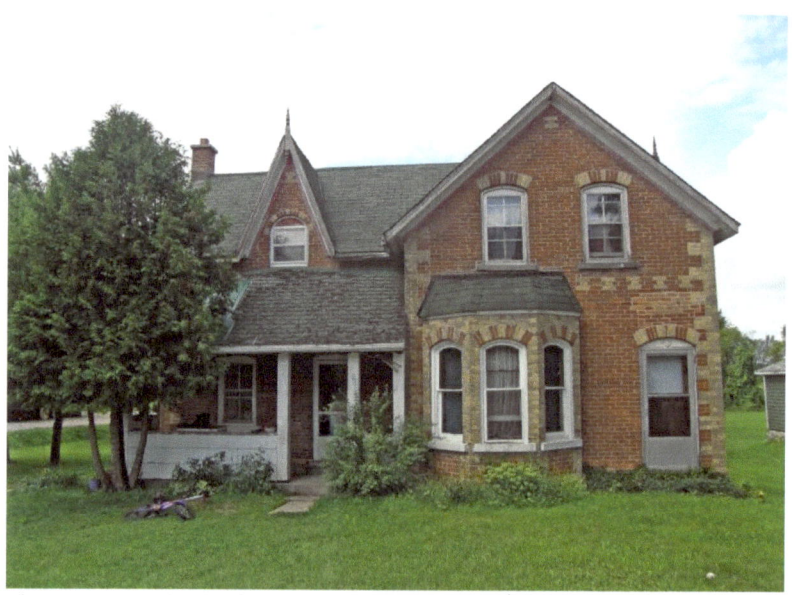

Gothic Revival, dichromatic brickwork, bay window, corner quoins, finial on small gable

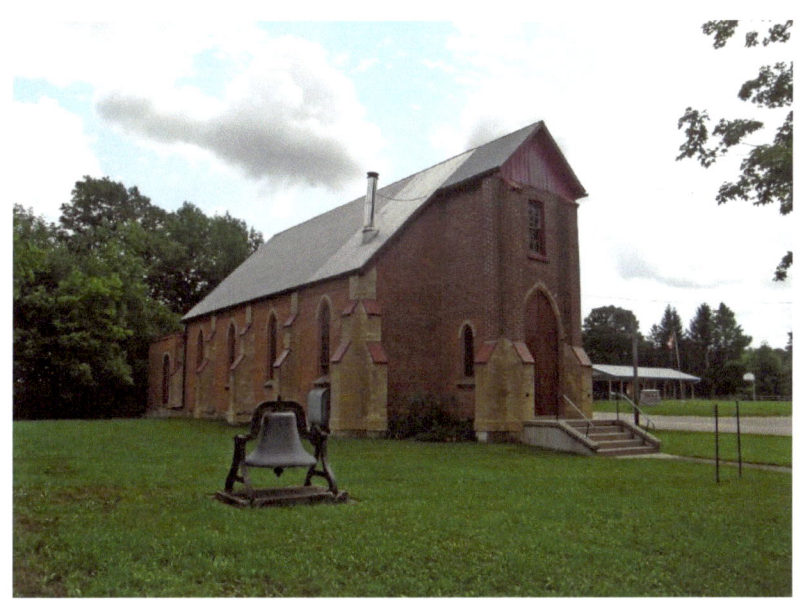

Buttresses, lancet windows

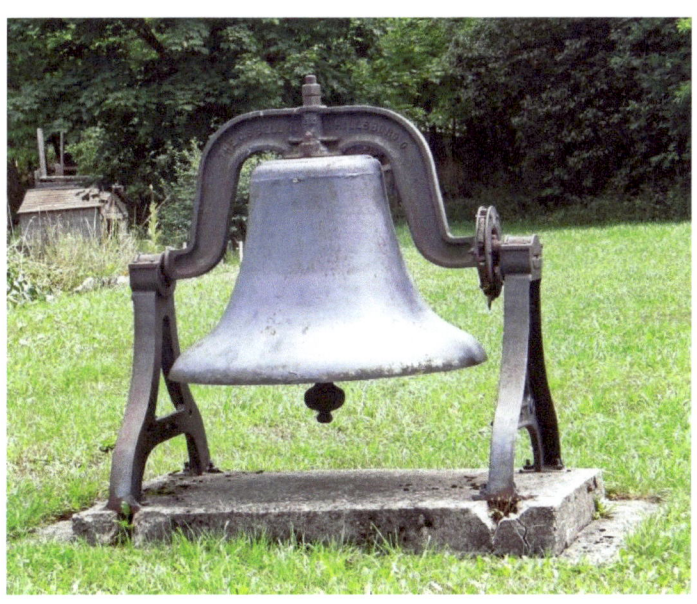

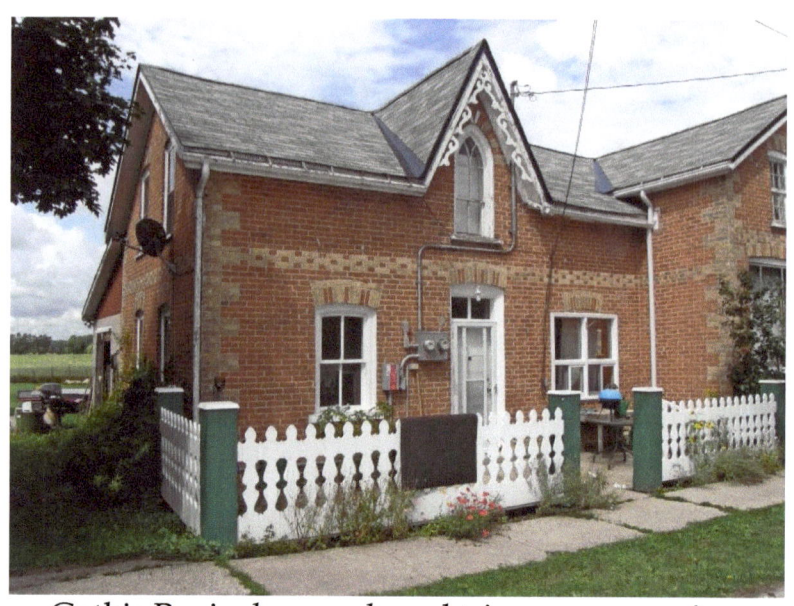

Gothic Revival, verge board trim, corner quoins, dichromatic brickwork, banding

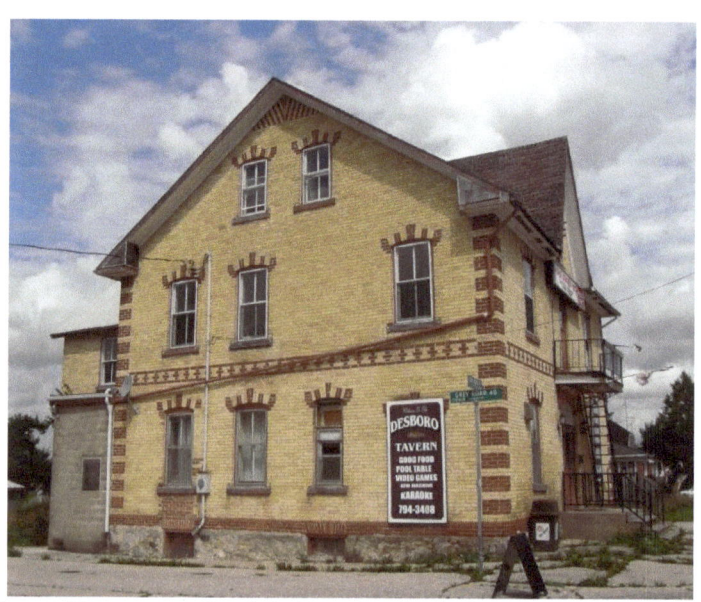

Desboro Tavern - Gothic Revival, dichromatic brickwork, corner quoins, banding

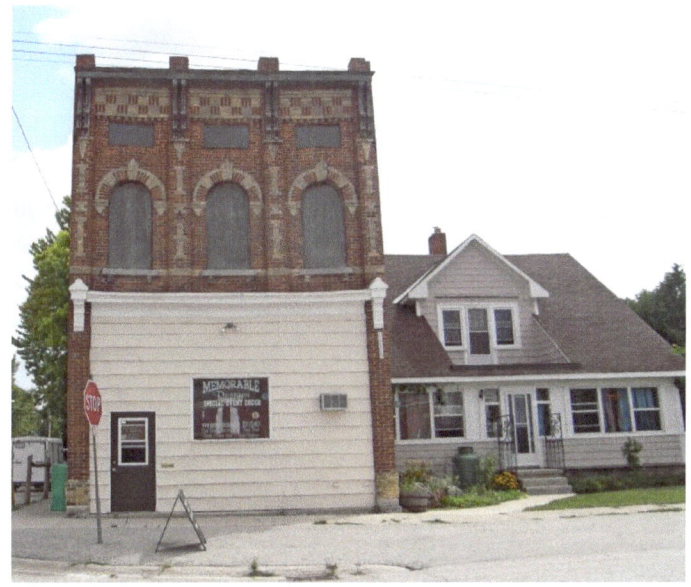

Concession 8 – dichromatic brickwork,
Window voussoirs with keystones

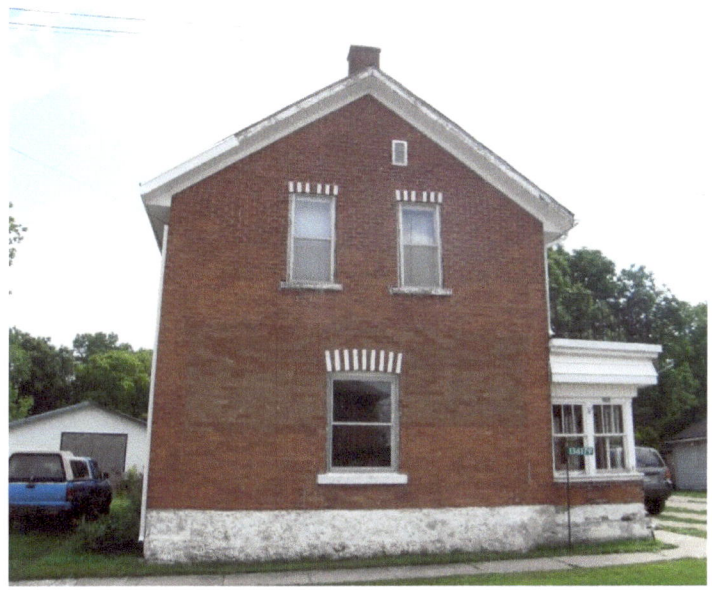

Gothic Revival

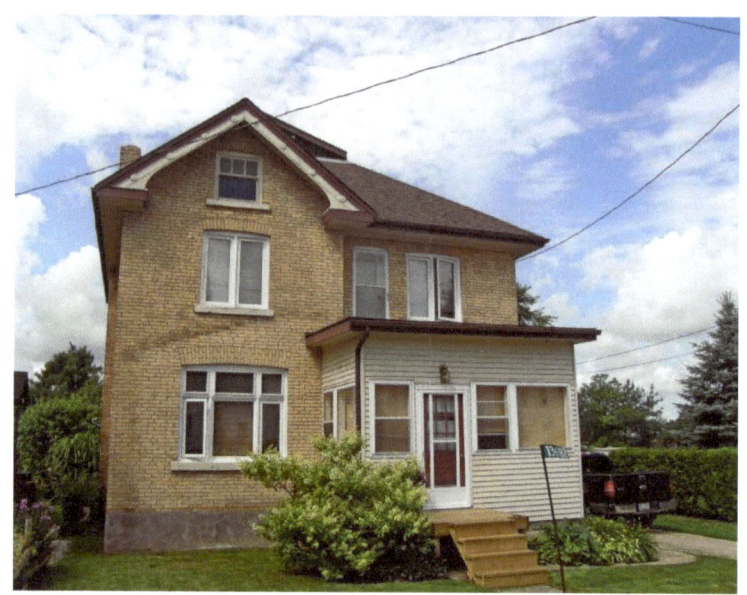

Gothic Revival – yellow brick

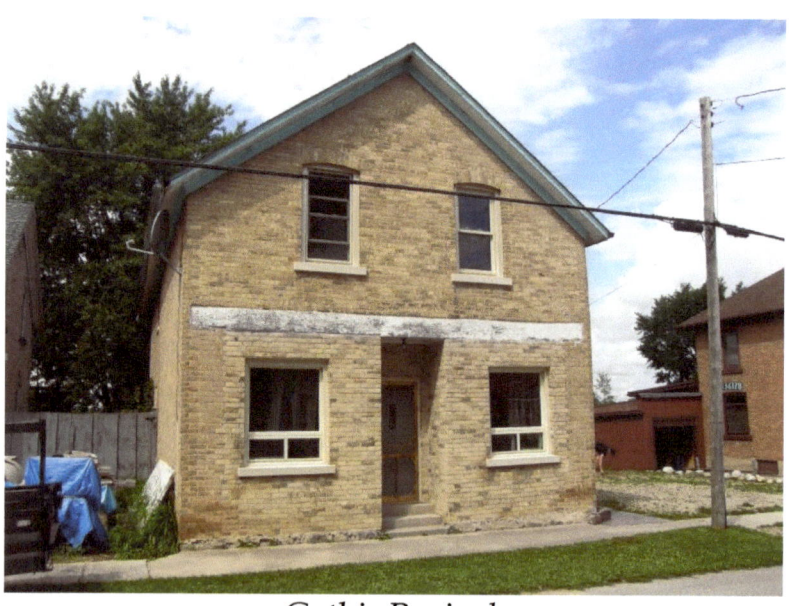

Gothic Revival

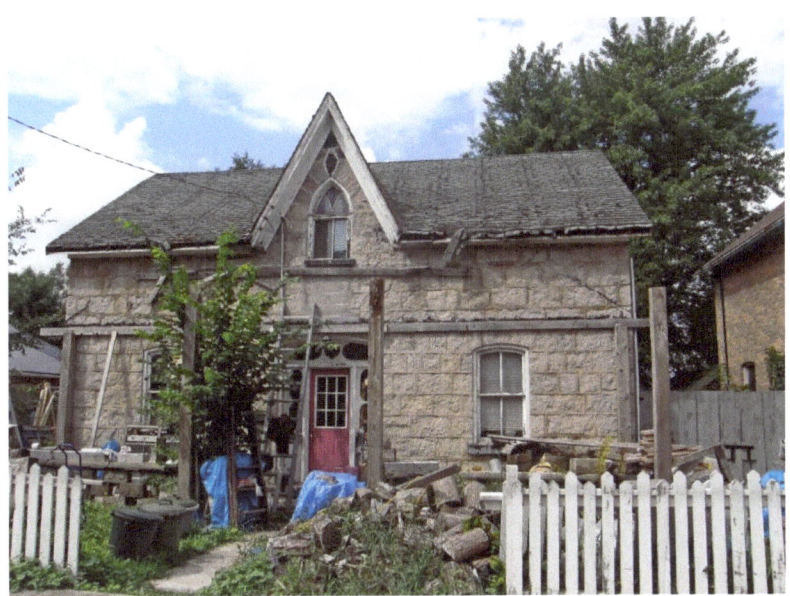

Gothic, limestone

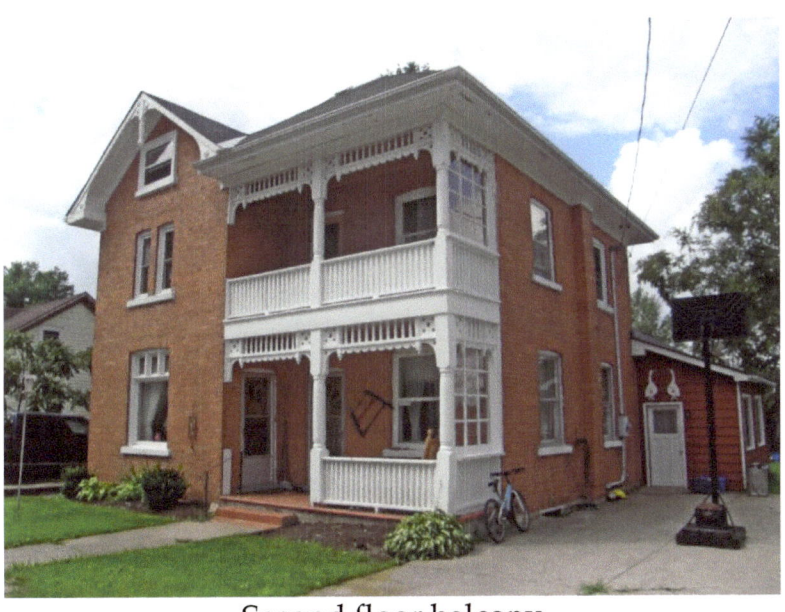

Second floor balcony

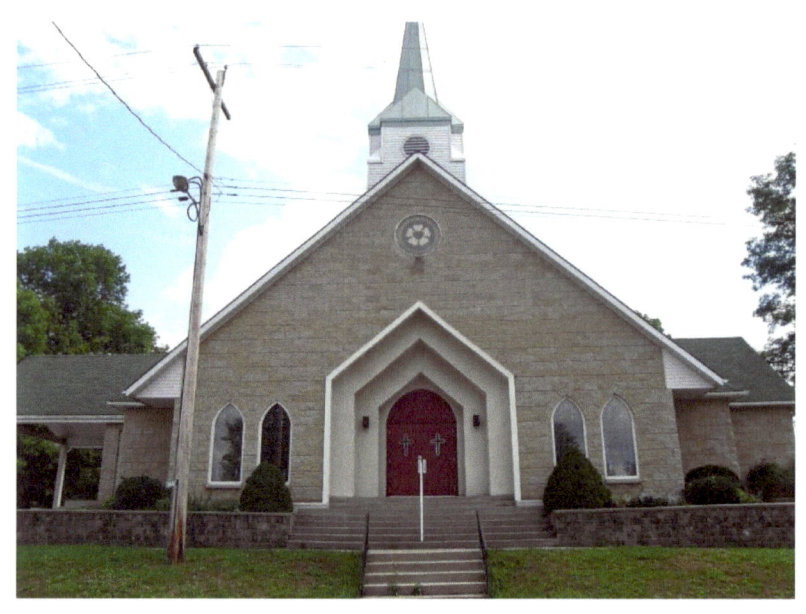

Faith Lutheran Church

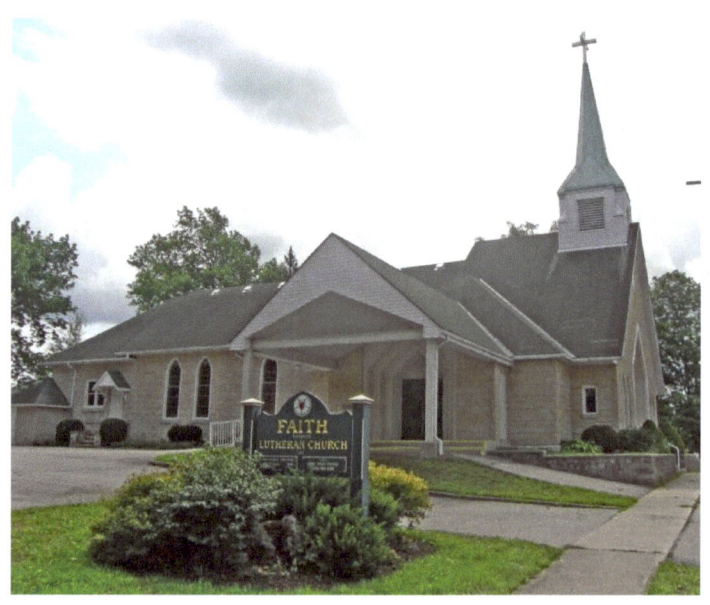

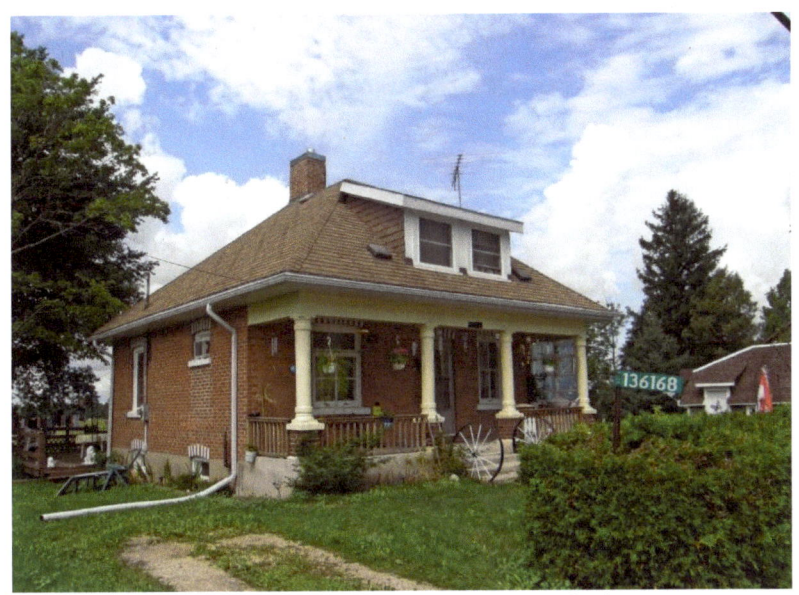

#136168 – Italianate, hipped roof, dormer

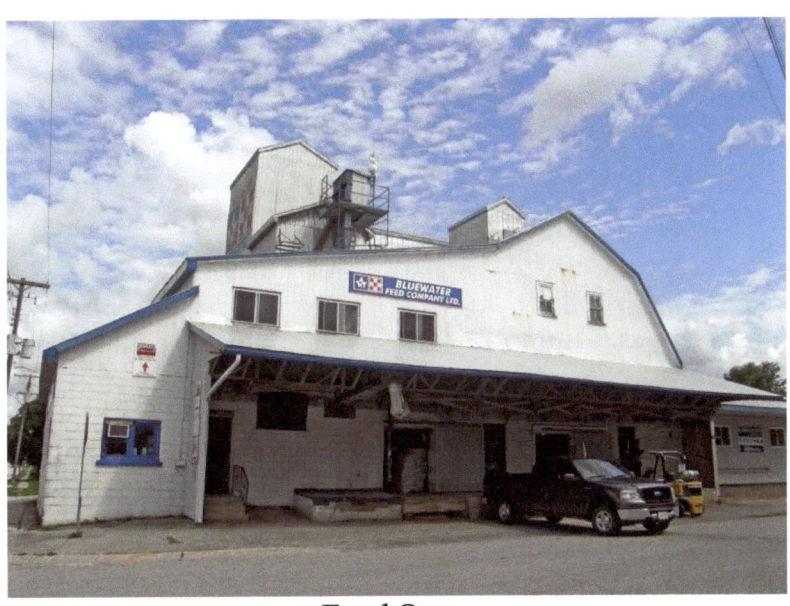

Feed Store

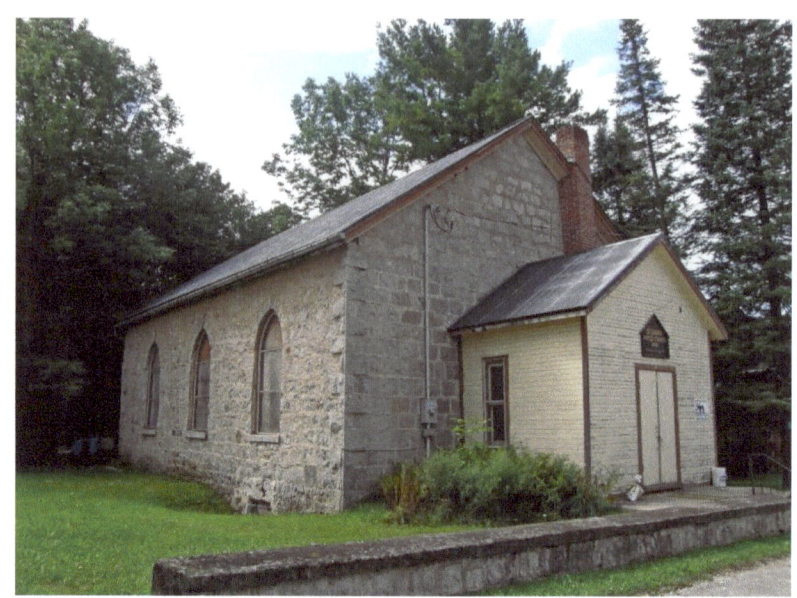

Desboro United Church 1876 - Gothic

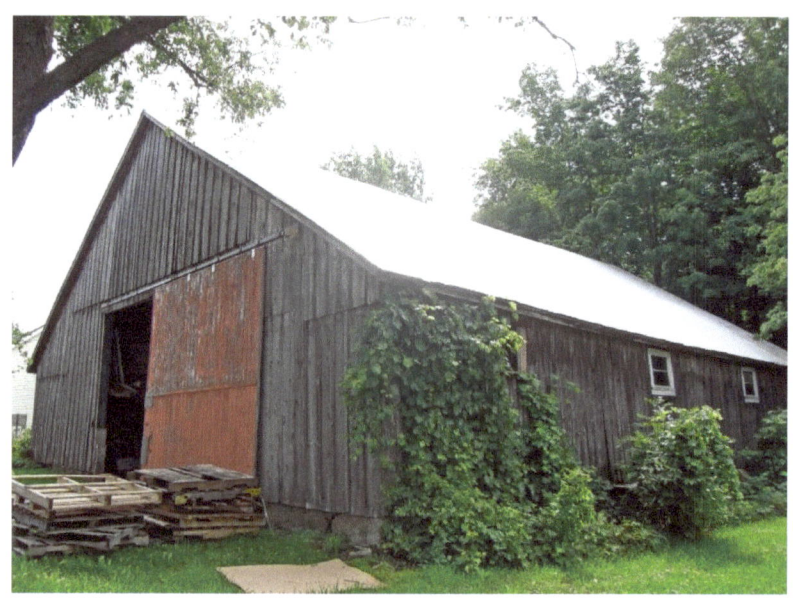

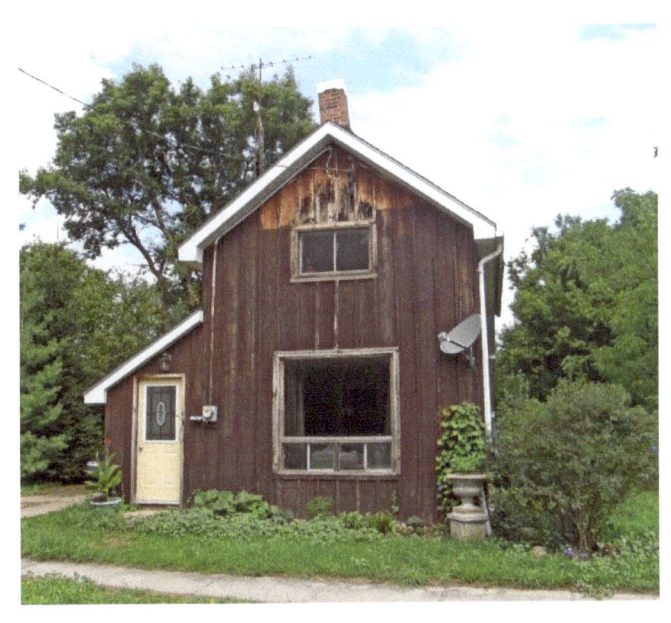

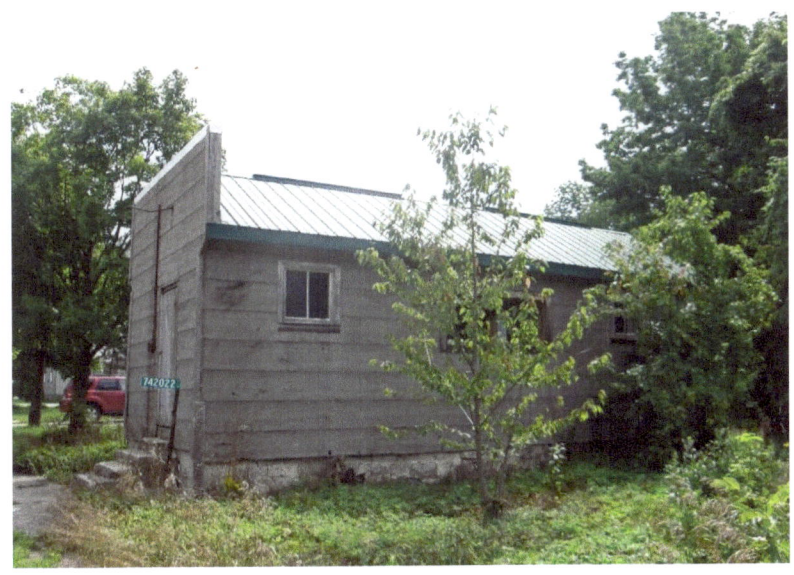

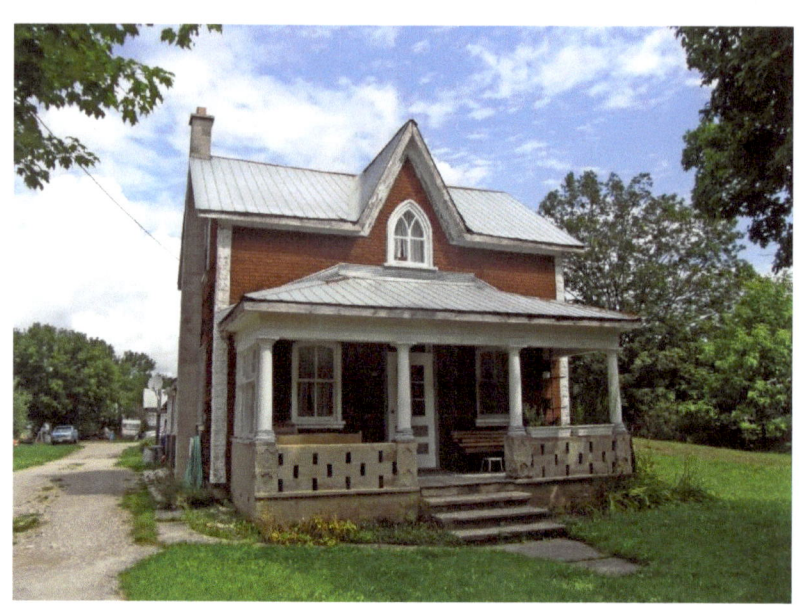

Gothic Revival

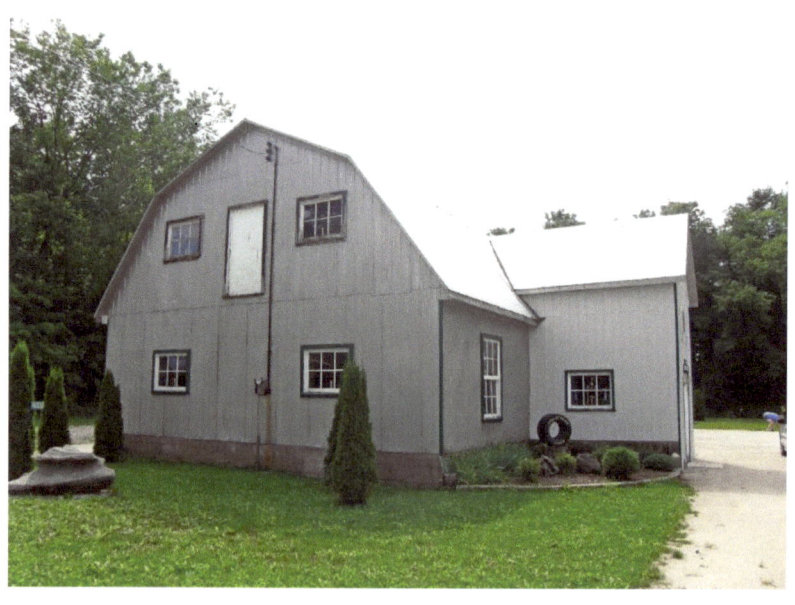

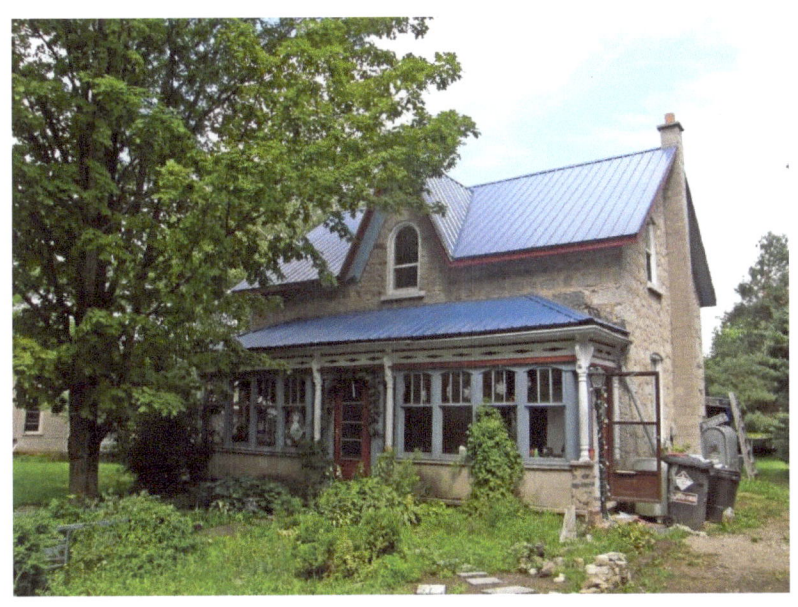

Gothic Revival

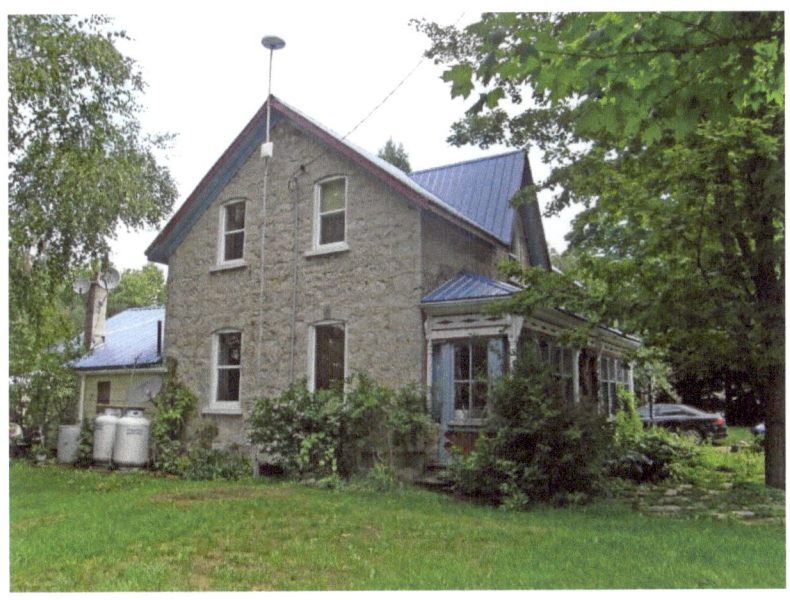

Grey Road 40 and 3

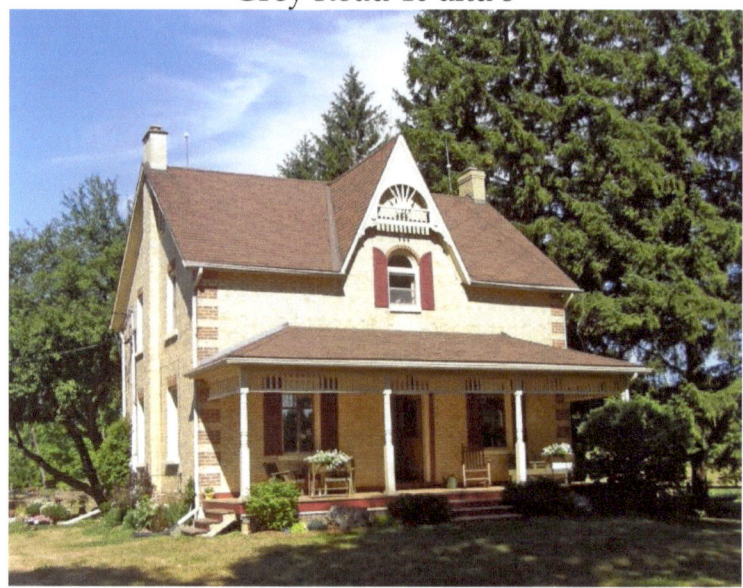

Gothic Revival, verge board trim on gable, corner quoins

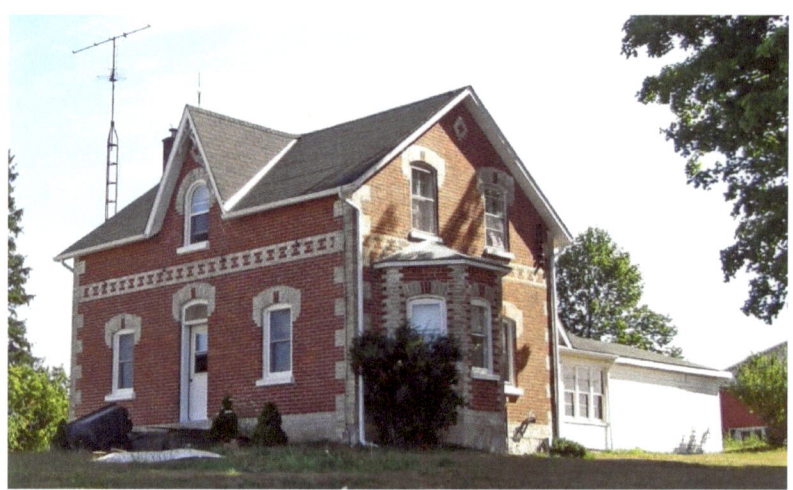

Gothic Revival, dichromatic brickwork, bay window, banding

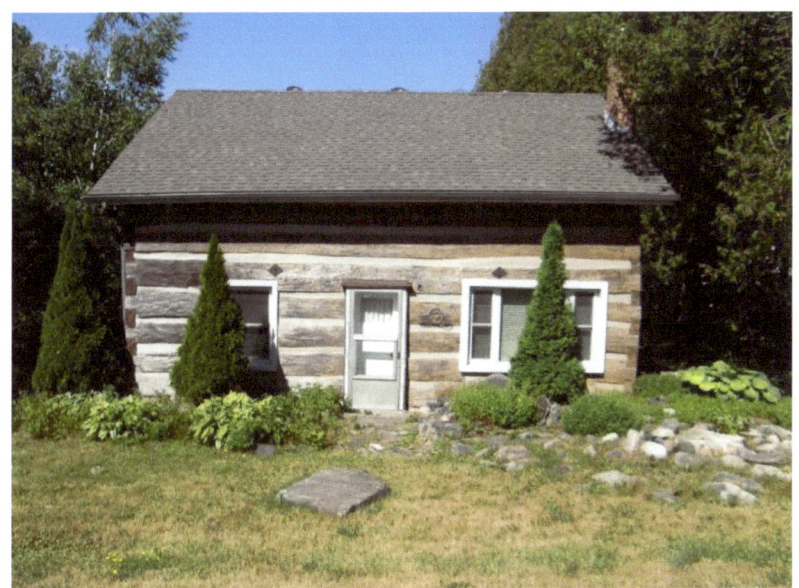

Log cabin

Marmion

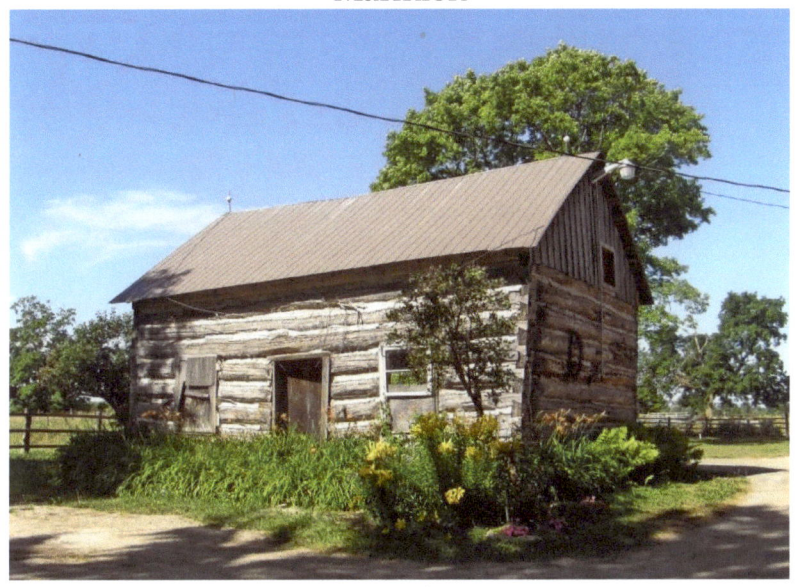

Log cabin

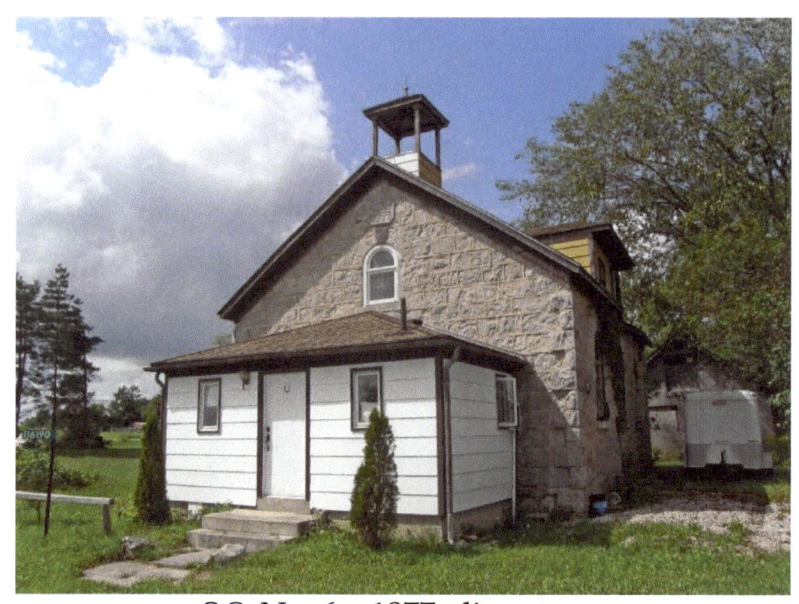

S.S. No. 6 – 1877 - limestone

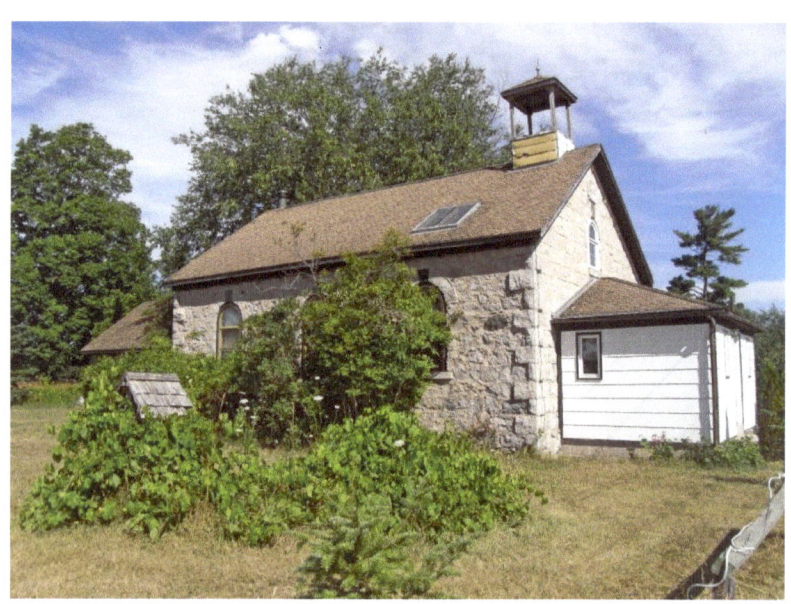

Gothic Revival - limestone – corner quoins

# Williamsford

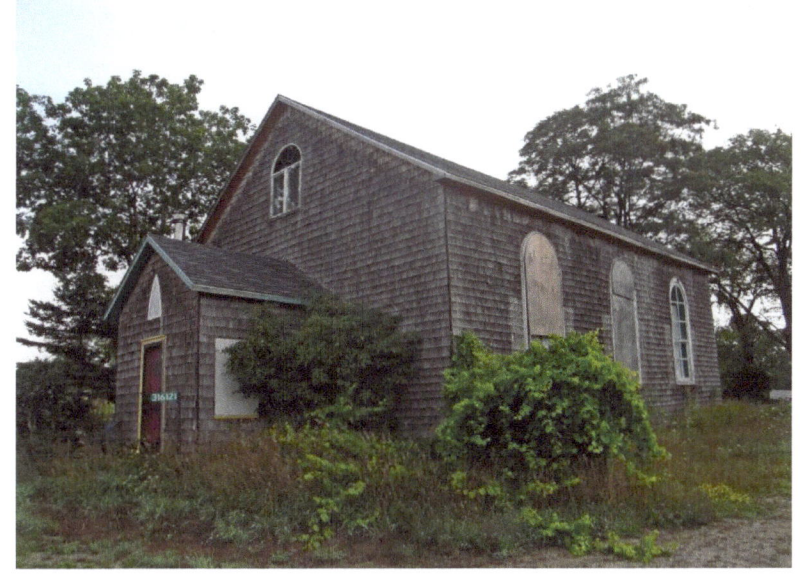

#316121

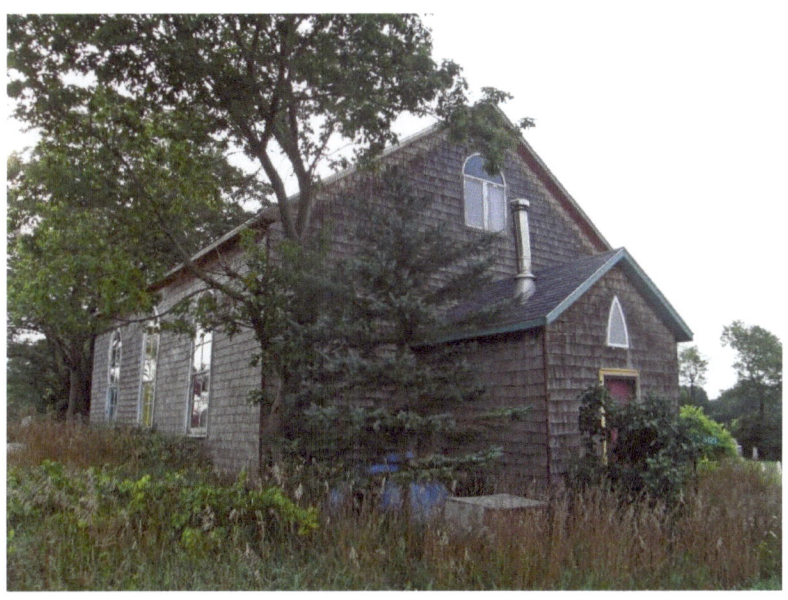

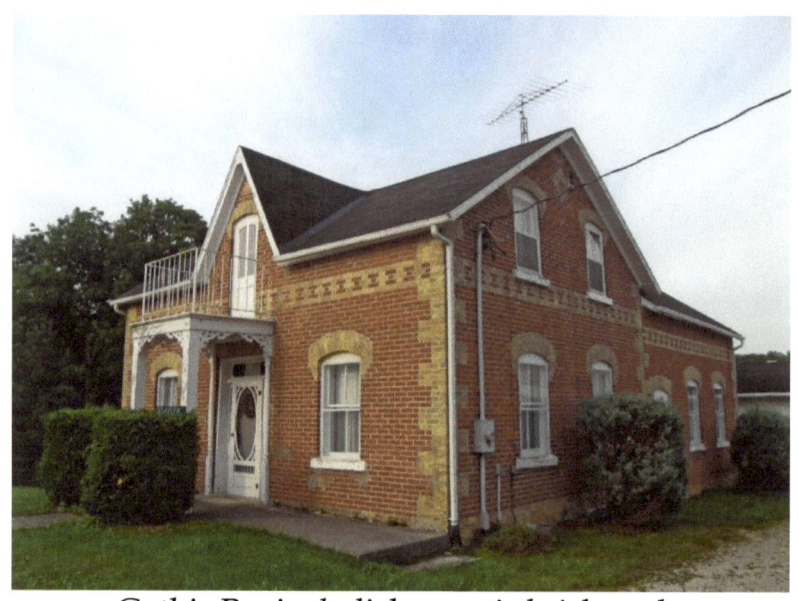

Gothic Revival, dichromatic brickwork,
corner quoins, 2nd floor balcony

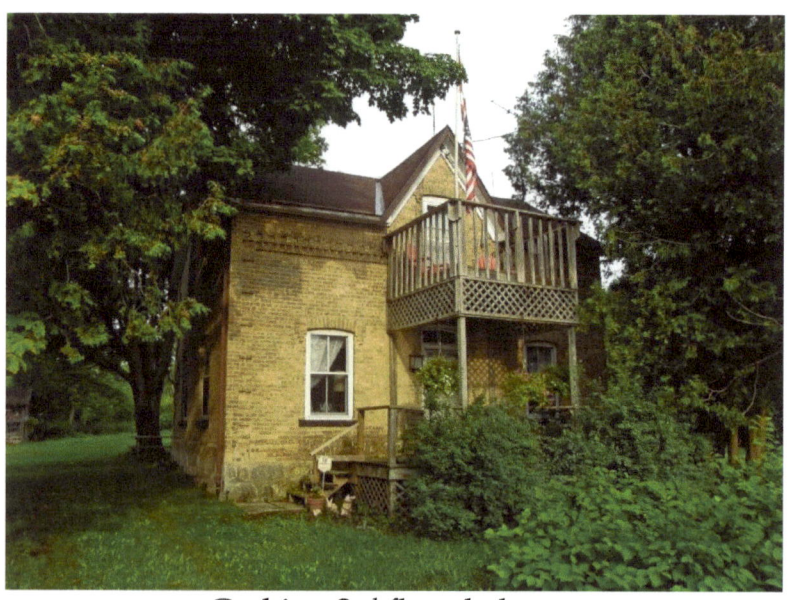

Gothic – 2nd floor balcony

Arkwright

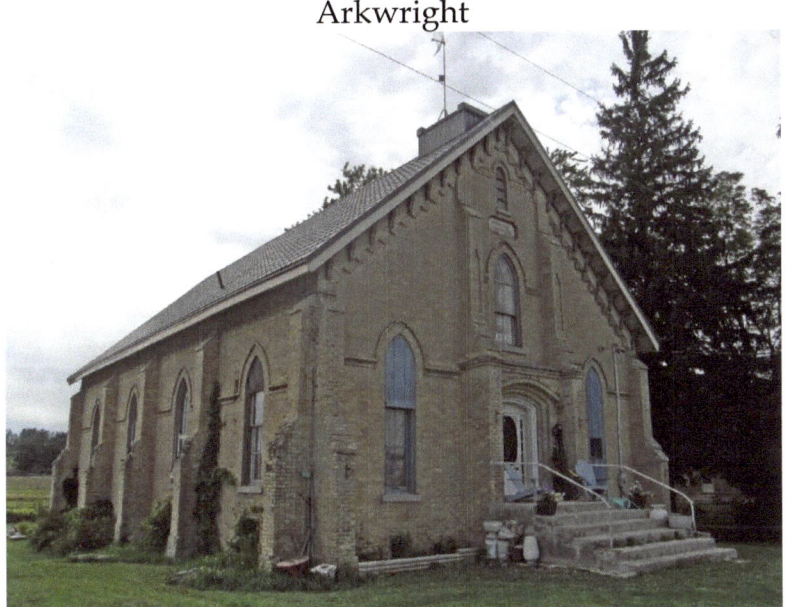

Arkwright United Church - bevelled dentil moulding,
buttresses, cornice brackets, lancet windows

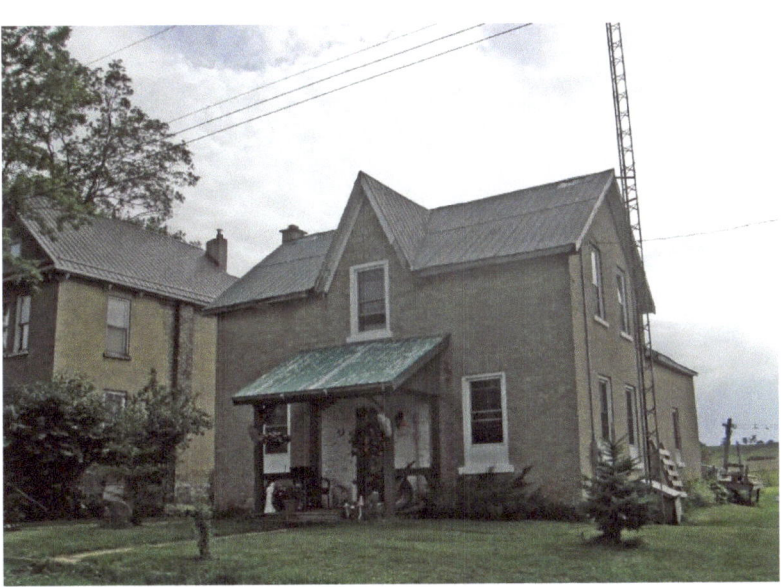

Gothic Revival

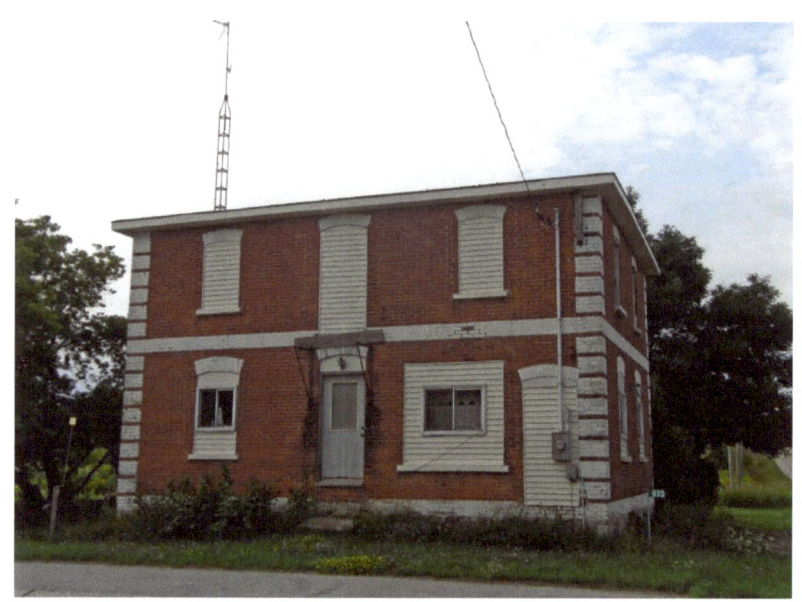

Corner quoins

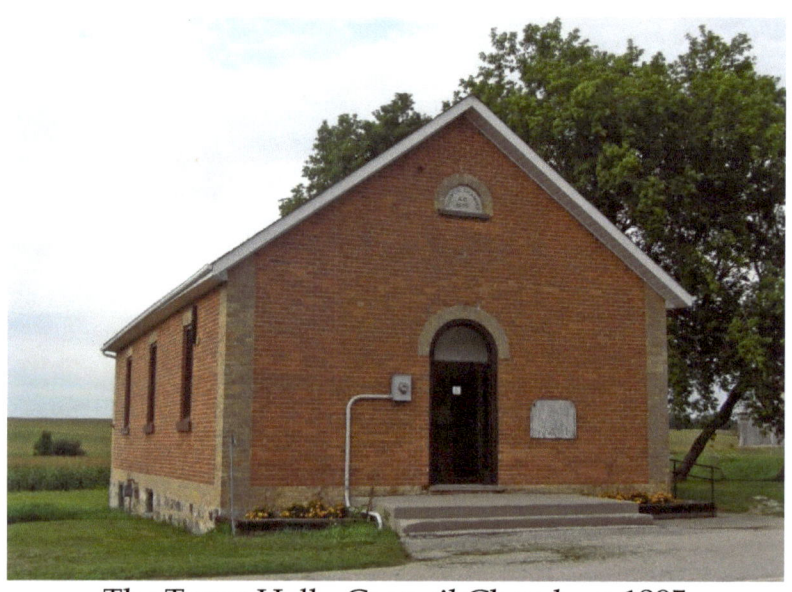

The Town Hall - Council Chambers 1895

Dobbinton

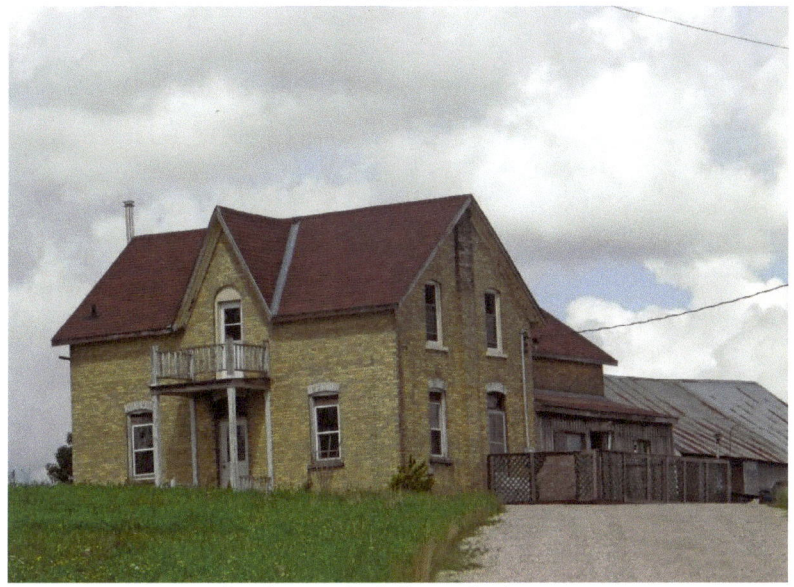

Gothic – 2nd floor balcony

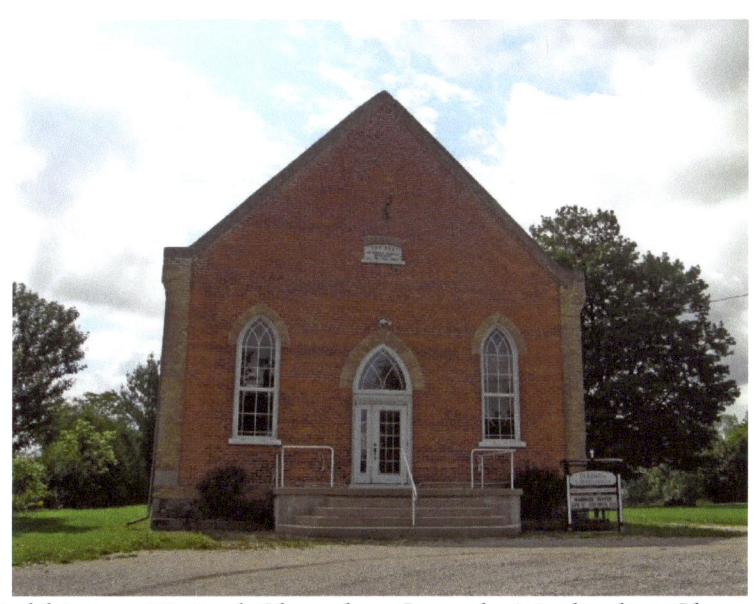

Dobbinton United Church – Canada Methodist Church
dedicated January 29 AD 1893

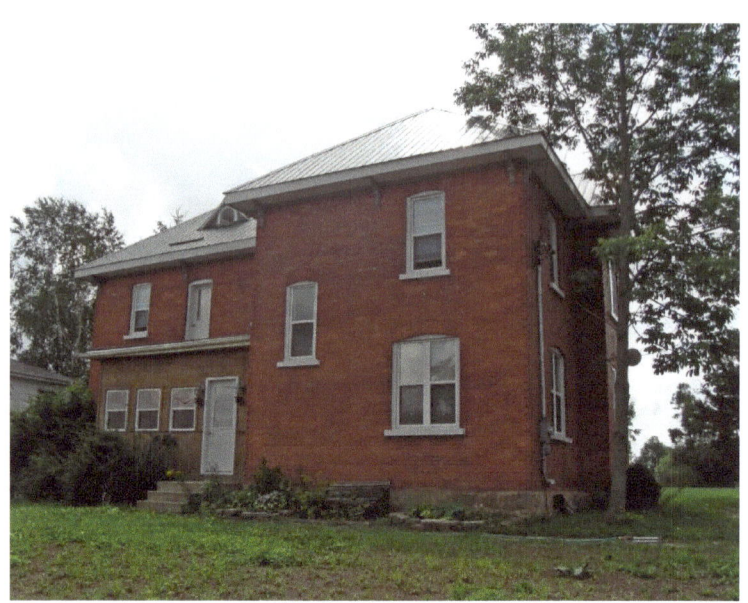

Hipped roof

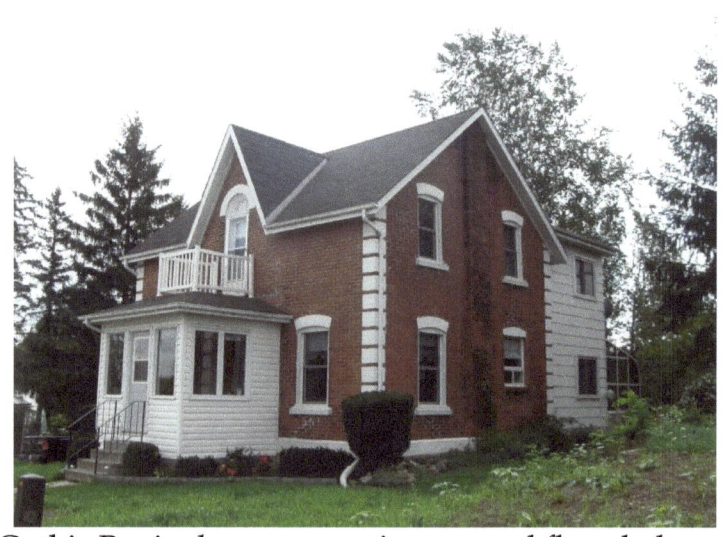

Gothic Revival, corner quoins, second floor balcony

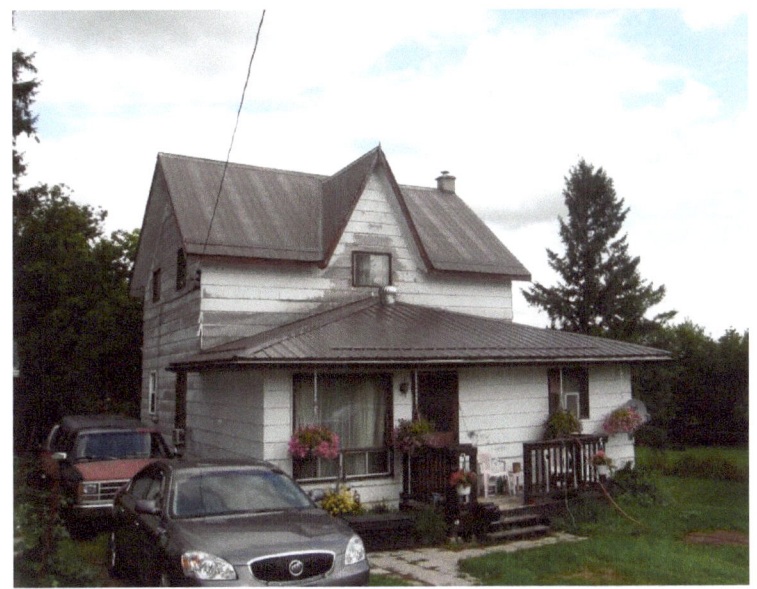

Gothic

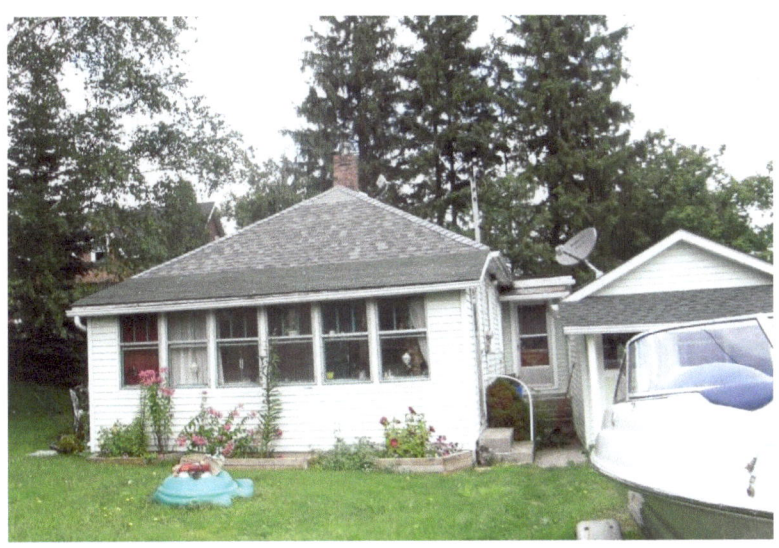

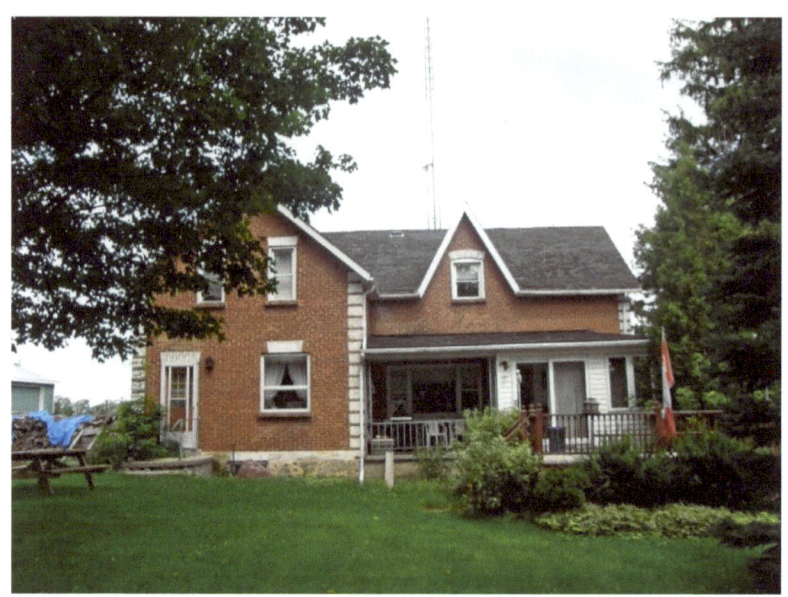

Gothic Revival, corner quoins

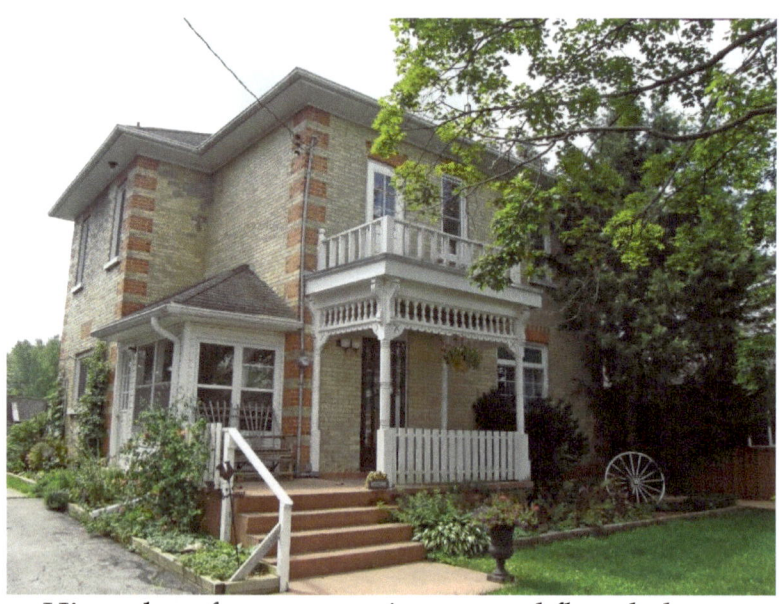

Hipped roof, corner quoins, second floor balcony

Keady

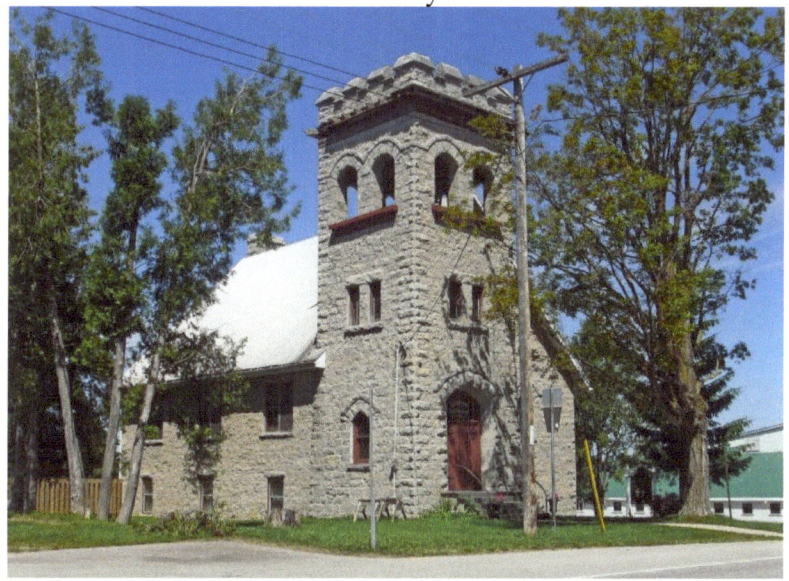

Chalmers Church, United Church of Canada, Keady

Tara

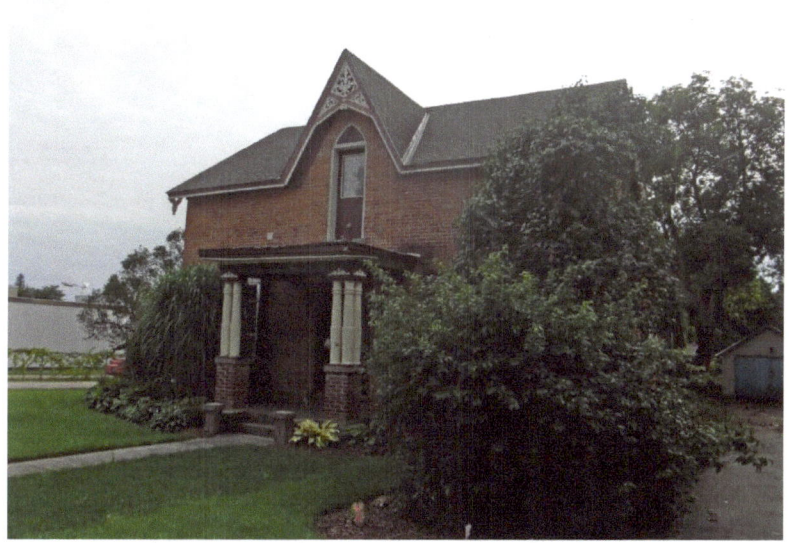

Gothic Revival, verge board trim on gable

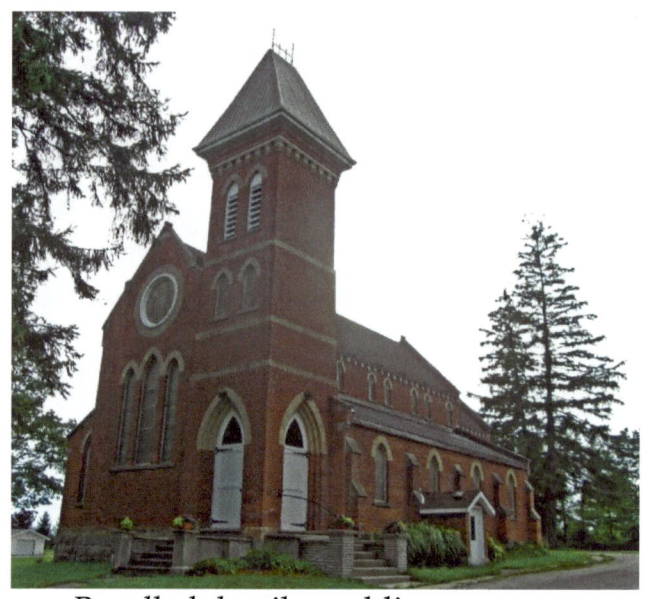

Bevelled dentil moulding on tower

Christ Church Anglican established 1877

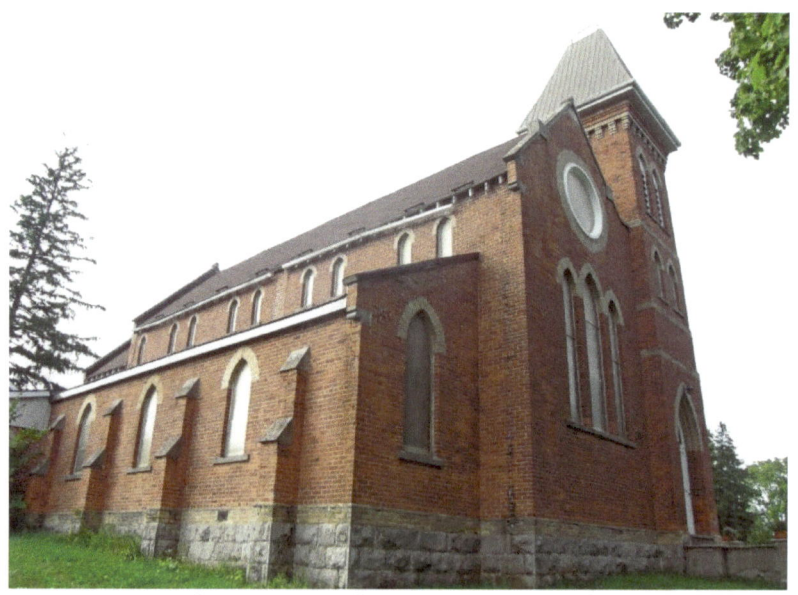

Buttresses, lancet windows, rose window, banding

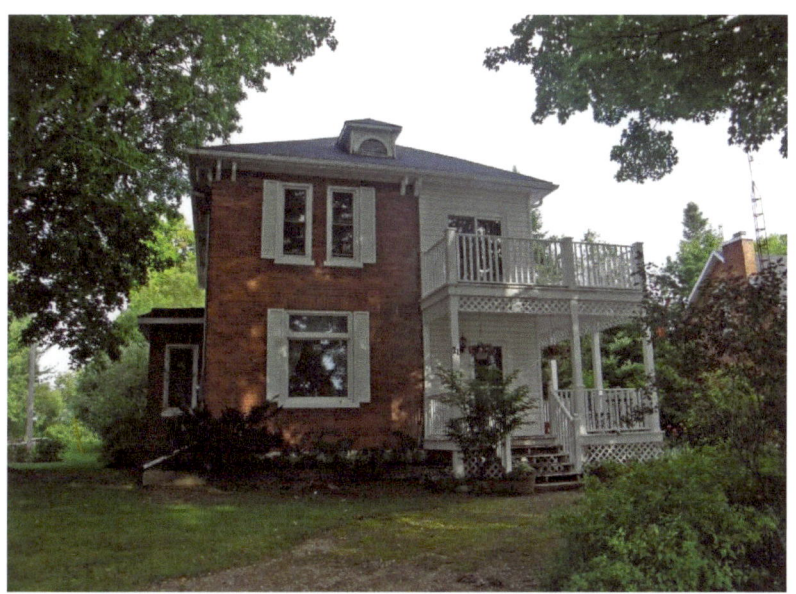

Italianate, hipped roof, second floor balcony

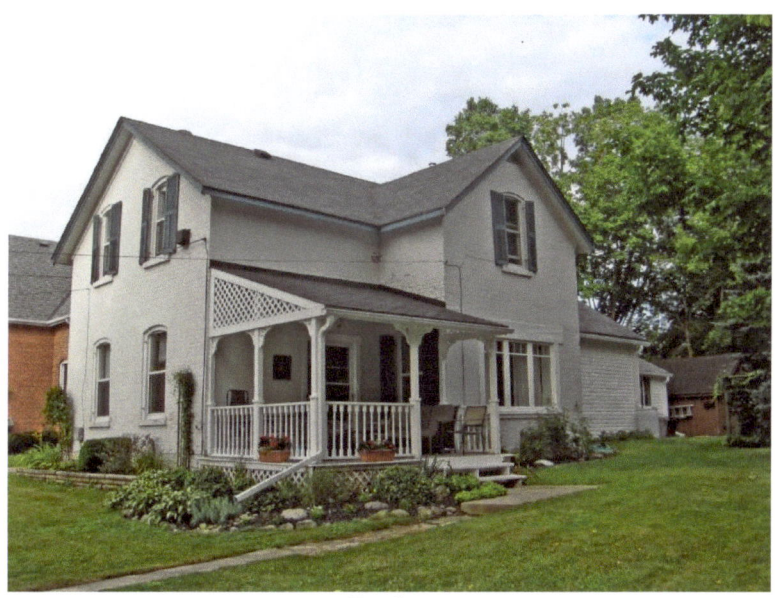

Gothic

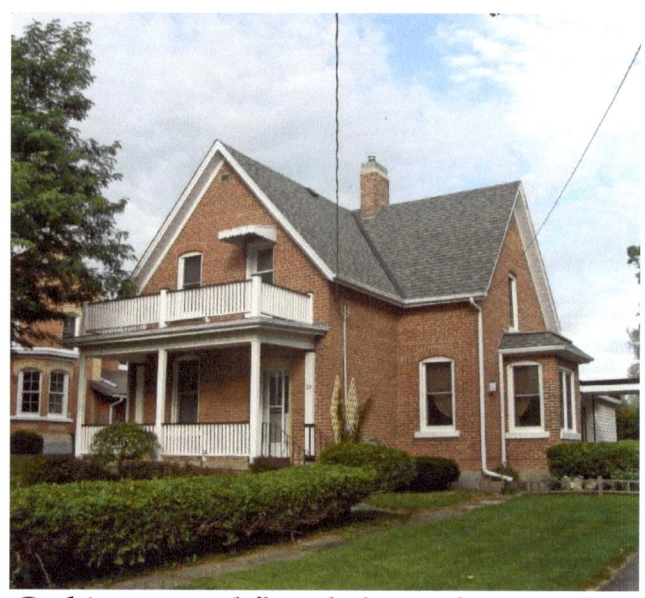

Gothic – second floor balcony, bay window

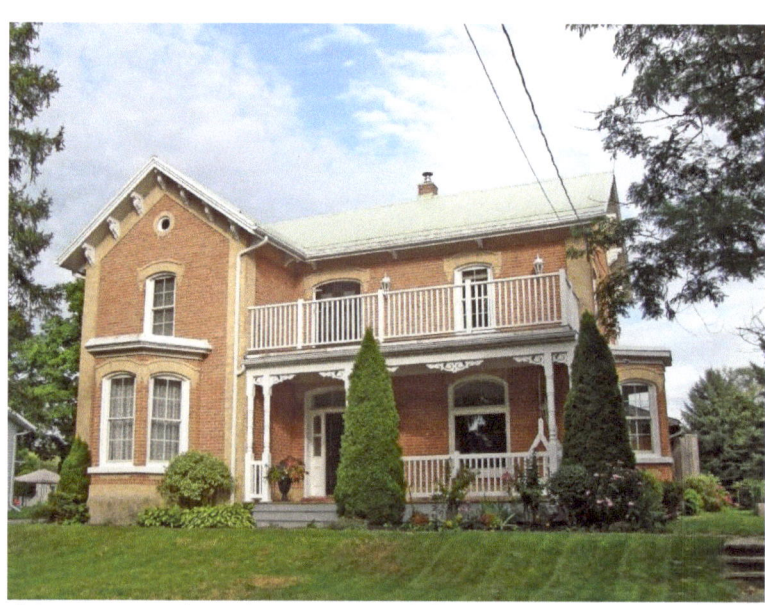

Gothic, cornice brackets, second floor balcony, bay window

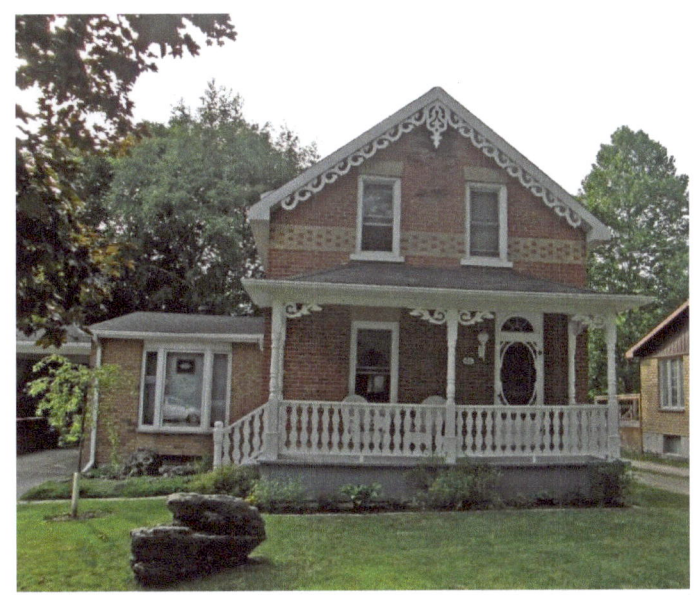

Gothic Revival, verge board trim and finial on gable

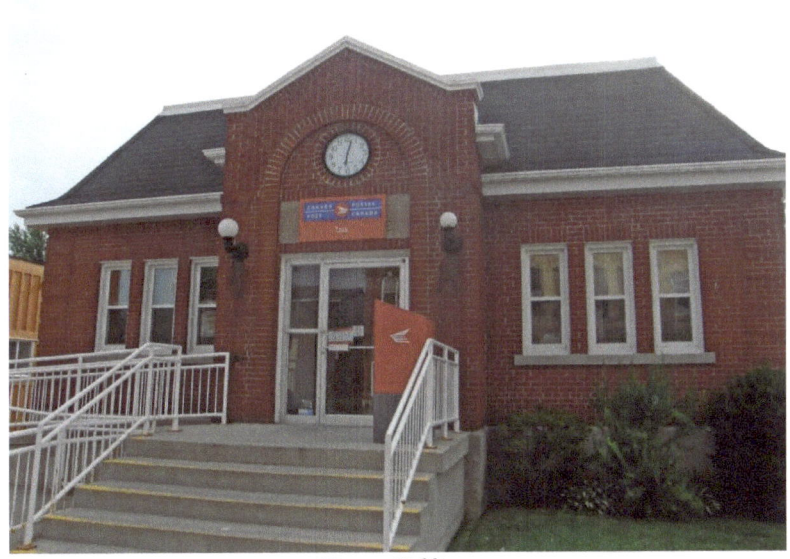

Post Office

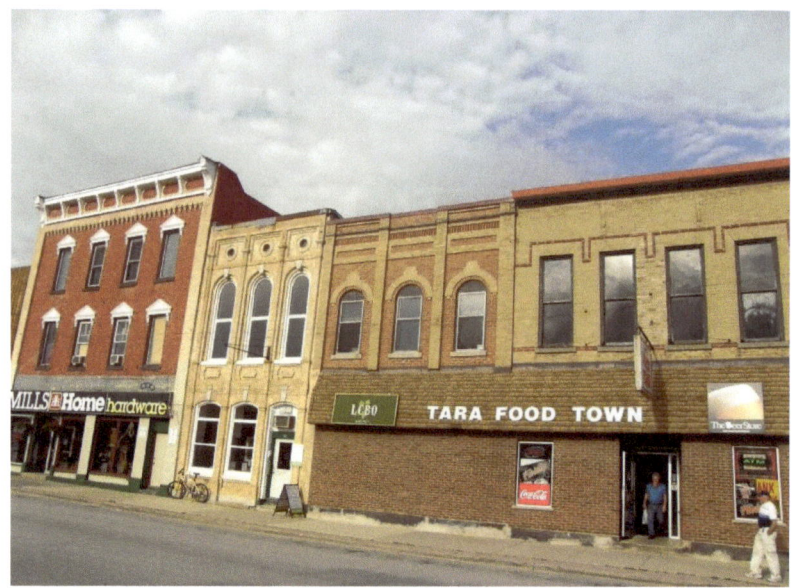

Voussoirs and keystones, brackets, banding, pilasters

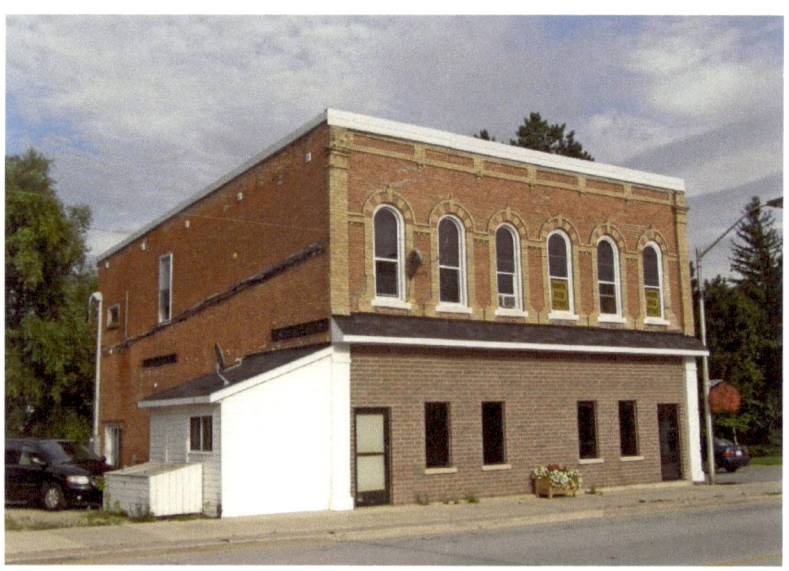

Dichromatic brickwork

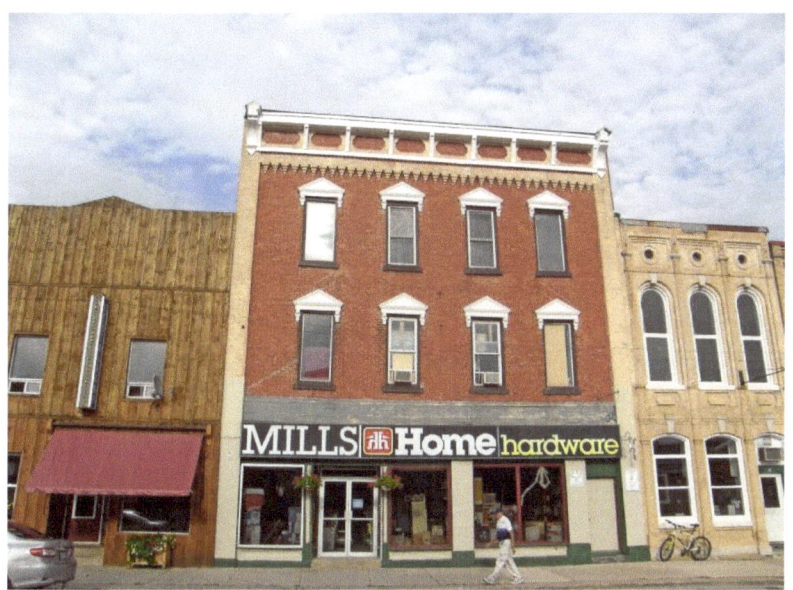

Dentil moulding, window hoods

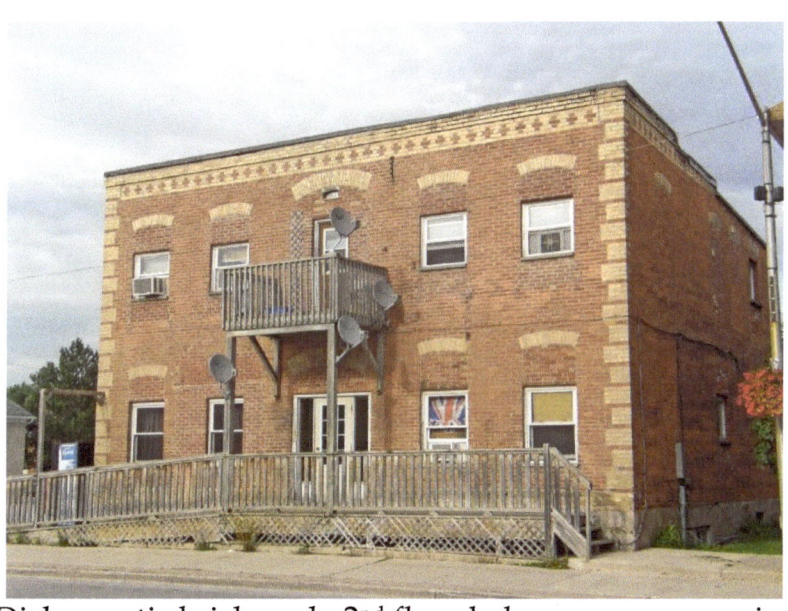

Dichromatic brickwork, 2nd floor balcony, corner quoins

# Williscroft

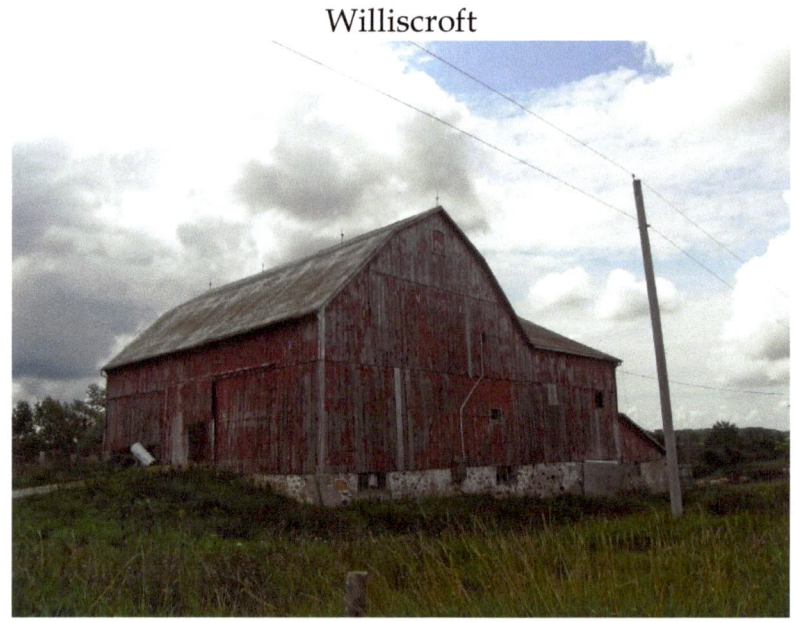

Cobblestone lower walls

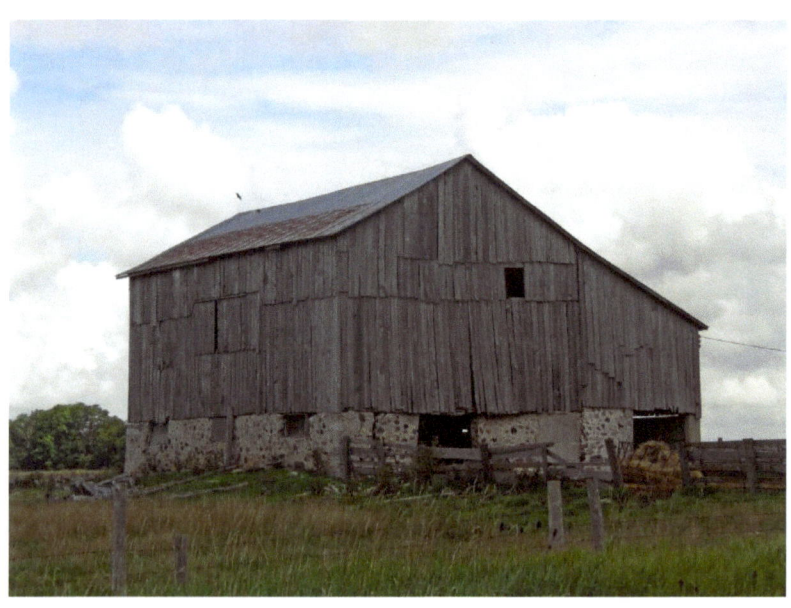

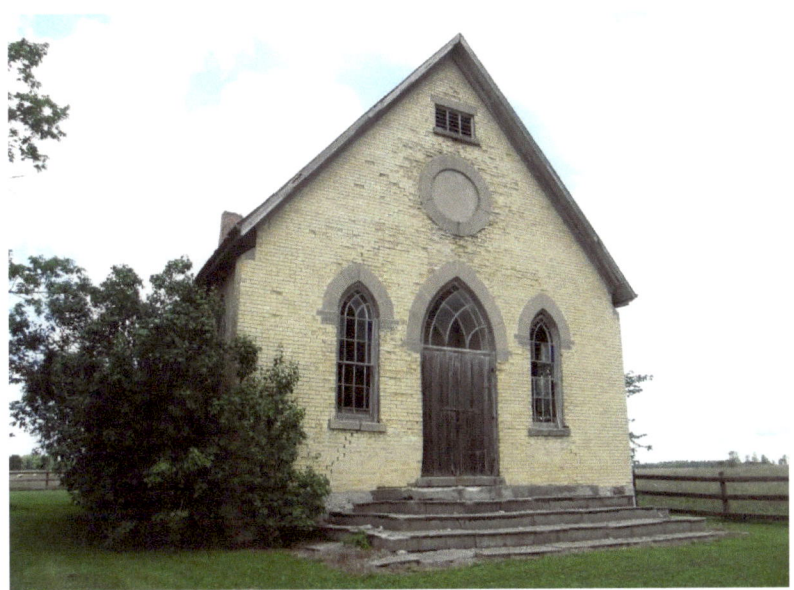

Baptist Church – Gothic, lancet windows

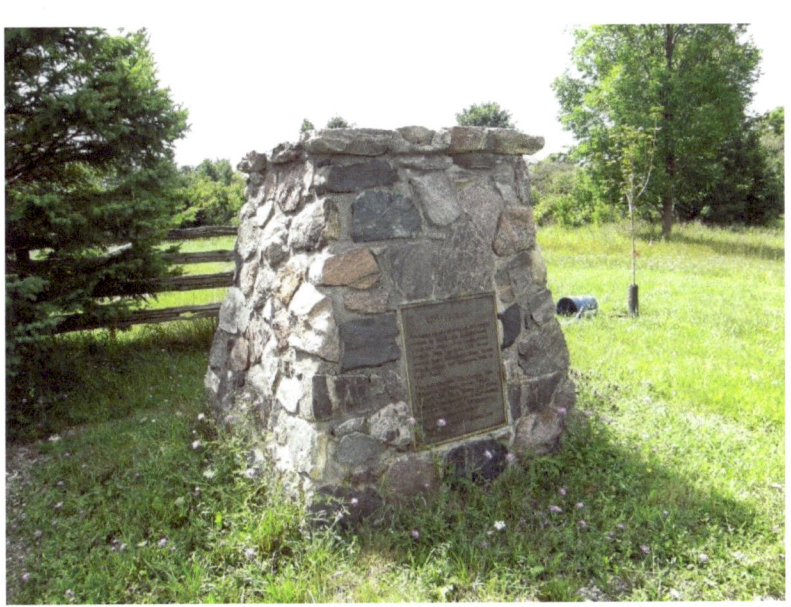

Williscroft cairn

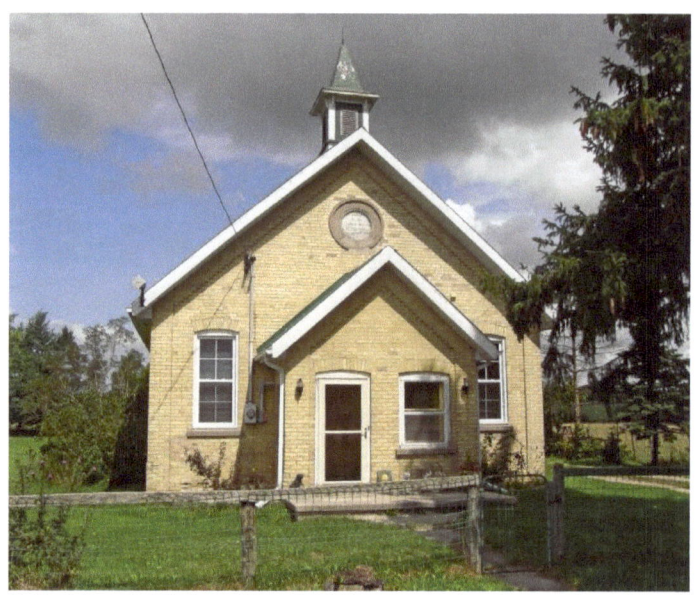

S.S. No. 8 Elderslie, 1907 – cupola for school bell

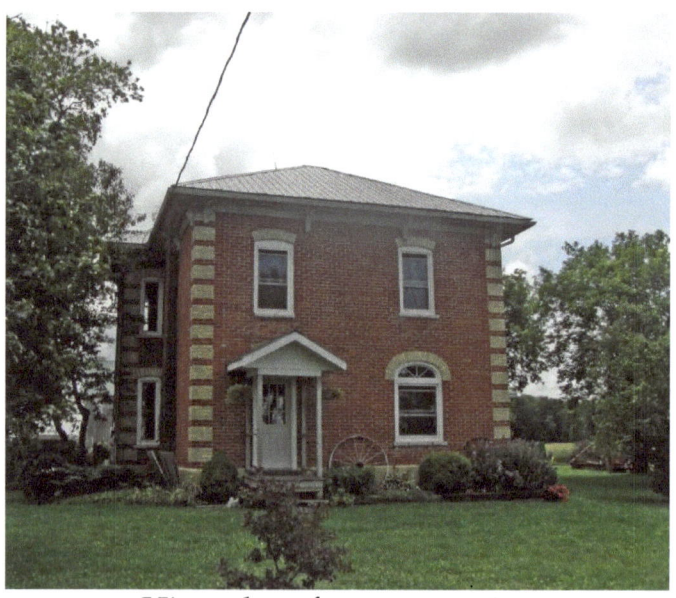

Hipped roof, corner quoins

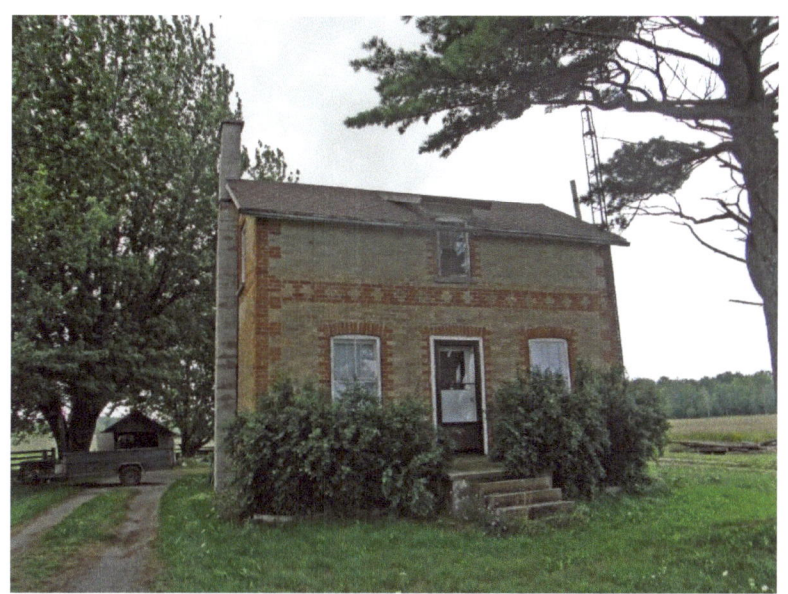

Dichromatic brickwork, corner quoins

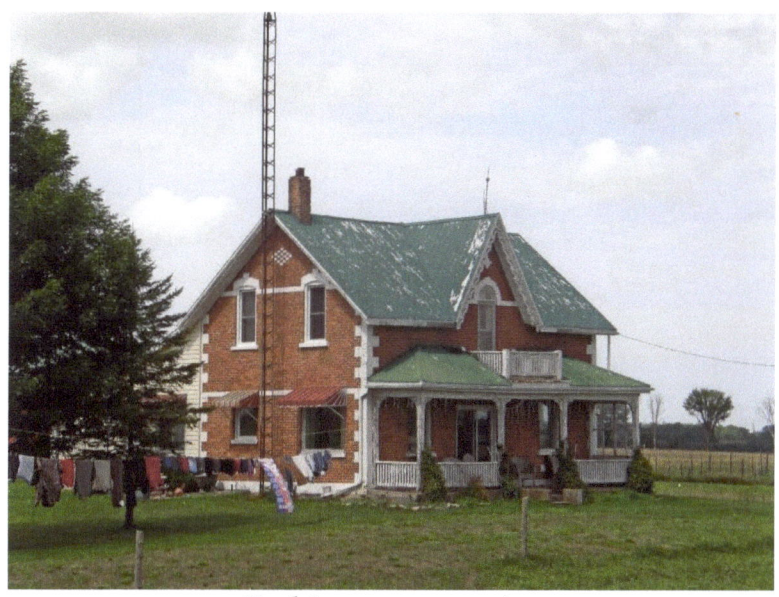

Gothic, corner quoins

# Architectural Terms

| | |
|---|---|
| **Banding**: Different materials, colours or textures used in horizontal bands along a wall.<br><br>Example: Desboro - see Page 23 | 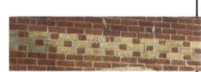 |
| **Bay Window:** A window that projects out from a wall, in a semicircular, rectangular, or polygonal design. Used frequently in Gothic and Victorian designs.<br>Example: Desboro – see Page 24 | 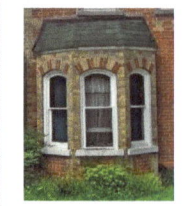 |
| **Brackets**: a decorative or weight-bearing structural element which forms a right angle with one side against a wall and the other under a projecting surface such as an eave or roof.<br>Example: see Page 27 | 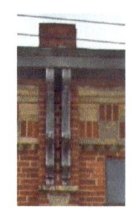 |
| **Buttress**: a masonry structure built against or projecting from a wall which serves to support or reinforce the wall.  In Canadian architecture, they are sometimes used for decoration.<br>Example: Desboro – see Page 25 | 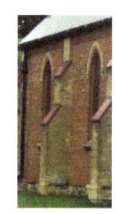 |
| **Cobblestone architecture: R**efers to the use of cobblestones embedded in mortar as a method for erecting walls on houses and commercial buildings.<br>Example: many examples including Pages 12-14 | 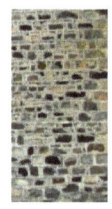 |

| | |
|---|---|
| **Cornice Return:** decorative element on the end of a gable.<br>Example: see Page 15 | 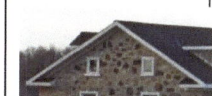 |
| **Dichromatic brickwork**: the use of two colours of brick, tile or slate to decorate a façade.<br>Example: see Page 27 | 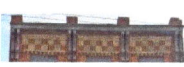 |
| **Dormer**: (French for "sleep") a gable end window that pierces through the plane of a sloping roof surface to create usable space in the top floor or attic of a building by adding headroom.<br>Example:  see Page 15 | 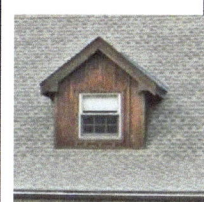 |
| **Gable**: the triangular portion of a wall between the edges of a sloping roof.<br><br>Example:  see Page 16 – birthplace of Prime Minister John Diefenbaker | 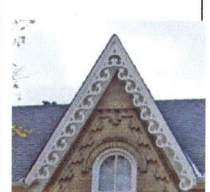 |
| **Hipped Roof**: a roof where all sides slope downwards to the walls with no gables.<br>Example: Desboro – see Page 31 | 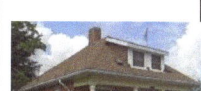 |
| **Keystones and Voussoirs**: a voussoir is a wedge-shaped element used in building an arch.  A keystone is the central stone that locks all the stones into position, allowing the arch to bear weight.  A keystone is often enlarged and embellished. Example: see Page 27 | 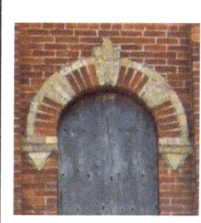 |

| | |
|---|---|
| **Lancet Window**: a tall, narrow window with a pointed arch at its top.<br><br>Example: see Page 17 | |
| **Pediment**: a triangular section above the horizontal structure (entablature), typically supported by columns. The inside of the triangle is called the tympanum.<br>Example: see Page 19 | |
| **Pilaster**: a slightly projecting column built into or applied to the face of a wall for additional structural support.<br><br>Example: see Page 27 | |
| **Quoin**: masonry blocks at the corner of a wall, often a decorative feature, usually larger or of a different colour than the rest of the wall.<br><br>Example: see Page 10 | |
| **Rose Window:** a circular window with ornamental tracery radiating from the centre.<br><br>Example: Tara Christ Church, see Page 48 | |
| **Verge board and Finial**: also called bargeboards – hang from the projecting end of a roof and are often elaborately carved and ornamented. **Finial:** ornament added to the top of a gable, pinnacle, canopy or spire – a Gothic element. Example: see Page 17<br>Finial: see Page 24 | |

# Building Styles

| | |
|---|---|
| Gothic Revival, 1830-1890 – These decorative buildings have sharply-pitched gables with highly detailed verge boards, pointed-arch window openings, and dichromatic brickwork. It is a common style in Ontario. Example: see Page 17 | |
| Italianate, 1850-1900 – It has wide-bracketed eaves, belvederes, wrap-around verandahs.<br><br>Example: see Page 10 | |
| A log cabin, built from logs, was usually one- or 1½-storeys constructed with round rather than hewn, or hand-worked, logs, and erected quickly for frontier shelter.  Log cabins were built from logs laid horizontally and interlocked on the ends with notches.  The cabin was situated to provide sunlight and drainage so the pioneers could cope better with the rigors of frontier life.  Careful notching minimized the size of the gap between the logs and reduced the amount of chinking with sticks and rocks or daubing with mud to fill the gap. The length of one log was the length of one wall.  Grey Road 40 and 3 – see Page 37 | |
| Tudor Revival – exposed timbers with stucco infill, multi-paned windows.<br><br>Example: see Page 18 | |